THE COMPLETE GUIDE TO **PHOTOSHOP'S** MOST

LAYERS

Matt Kloskowski

**The Layers
Book Team**

CREATIVE DIRECTOR
Felix Nelson

ASSOCIATE ART DIRECTOR
Jessica Maldonado

TECHNICAL EDITORS
Kim Doty
Cindy Snyder

TRAFFIC DIRECTOR
Kim Gabriel

PRODUCTION MANAGER
Dave Damstra

COVER PHOTOS
COURTESY OF
iStockphoto.com

PUBLISHED BY
Peachpit Press

Composed in Avenir and Army Thin by Kelby Media Group, Inc.

Trademarks
All terms mentioned in this book that are known to be trademarks or service marks have been appropriately capitalized. Peachpit Press cannot attest to the accuracy of this information. Use of a term in the book should not be regarded as affecting the validity of any trademark or service mark.

Photoshop is a registered trademark of Adobe Systems Incorporated.
Macintosh is a registered trademark of Apple, Inc.
Windows is a registered trademark of Microsoft Corporation.

Warning and Disclaimer
This book is designed to provide information about Photoshop. Every effort has been made to make this book as complete and as accurate as possible, but no warranty of fitness is implied.

The information is provided on an as-is basis. The author and Peachpit Press shall have neither the liability nor responsibility to any person or entity with respect to any loss or damages arising from the information contained in this book or from the use of the discs or programs that may accompany it.

THIS PRODUCT IS NOT ENDORSED OR SPONSORED BY ADOBE SYSTEMS INCORPORATED, PUBLISHER OF PHOTOSHOP.

ISBN 10:   0-321-74958-8
ISBN 13: 978-0-321-74958-1

9 8 7 6 5 4 3 2 1

Printed and bound in the United States of America

www.kelbytraining.com
www.peachpit.com

To my wife Diana:
For your unconditional love and dedication
to me, and to our family. For always making
me laugh. For listening when I just need to talk.
But most of all, for being the most caring, fun-
loving wife and best friend a guy could hope for.

fx

Of course, there are many people behind the scenes that helped make this book happen. One of my favorite parts of writing a book is that I get to thank them publicly in front of the thousands and thousands of people who read it. So here goes:

To my wife, Diana: No matter what the day brings, you always have a smile on your face when I come home. I could never thank you enough for juggling our lives and being such a great mom to our kids.

To my oldest son, Ryan: Your inquisitive personality amazes me and I love the little talks that we have. Thanks for being such a patient subject when I'm testing out photo gear and, most of all, thanks for kicking my butt at *Modern Warfare 2* on the Xbox 360. There's nothing like a dad coming home to a chopper gunner attack on him.

To my youngest son, Justin: I have no doubt that you'll be the class clown one day. No matter what I have on my mind, you always find a way to make me smile. That was just what I needed when working on this book.

To my mom and dad for giving me such a great start in life and always encouraging me to go for what I want.

To Ed, Kerry, Kristine, and Scott (my brothers and sisters) for supporting me and always giving me someone to look up to.

Thanks to Scott Kelby for having become a mentor and just all-around great friend. You'll never know how much that one lunch at Ruby Tuesday's helped me when writing this book. Thanks man!

To the folks that make this book look like the awesome book that you see: Felix Nelson, Jessica Maldonado, and Dave Damstra.

I owe a huge thank you to Nicole Procunier for making the cover image of this book totally rock, and for helping me out with many of the graphics and projects in the tutorials.

To my two favorite editors in the world: Cindy Snyder and Kim Doty. Thanks for making me look so good.

To Paul Wilder, our in-house IT guru, for making sure I have a great computer and the software I need, when I need it.

To Dave Moser, the business powerhouse behind Kelby Media Group. Your militaristic, yet insightful, comments throughout the day help me way more than you know. Thanks for continuing to push me to be better each day.

To Dave Cross, Corey Barker, and RC Concepcion for putting up with me asking them, "Hey guys, what do you think of this?" questions for a month while writing this book. You guys rock!

To all my friends at Peachpit Press: Ted Waitt, Scott Cowlin, Gary-Paul Prince, and Sara Jane Todd. It's because you guys are so good at what you do that I'm able to continue doing what I love to do.

To you, the readers. Without you, well…there would be no book. Thanks for your constant support in emails, phone calls, and introductions when I'm out on the road teaching. You guys make it all worth it.

Thank you.

— Matt Kloskowski

Matt Kloskowski

Matt Kloskowski is a Photoshop Guy whose books, videos, and classes have simplified the way thousands of people work on digital photos and images. Author of several best-selling books on Photoshop, Matt teaches Photoshop and digital photography techniques to tens of thousands of people around the world each year. He co-hosts the top-rated videocast *Photoshop User TV*, as well as *D-Town TV*—the photography videocast that's broken the mold when it comes to teaching photography. He's built a massive library of videos that appear in DVDs and online training courses, and has written articles for *Photoshop User* magazine. You'll find Matt teaching for the Kelby Training Live seminar tour, as well as at the world's premier Photoshop event, the Photoshop World Conference & Expo. Matt lives in Tampa, Florida, and works at the National Association of Photoshop Professionals.

CHAPTER SEVEN: RETOUCHING WITH LAYERS   179

CHAPTER EIGHT: LAYER STYLES   205

CHAPTER NINE: SMART LAYERS   227

CHAPTER TEN: ADVANCED LAYER BLENDING AND COMPOSITING   249

INTRODUCTION

You know what? I can't stand introductions. Weird coming from an author, right? It's like some committee got together and said that you've got to have an introduction in your book. Oh, and please make it long. Really long! In fact, make it so long that it will ensure no one reads introductions. And the vicious cycle begins. That said, I understand the concept of an introduction. It's for the author to introduce you to the content of the book and give you an idea of how best to get the most out of the book you just purchased. I'm going to do that, but I'm going to do it with a very short list (I love lists, by the way). Here goes:

1. If you want to follow along with the images used in the book, then feel free to download them at **www.kelbytraining.com/books/layerscs5**. You'll notice that most are watermarked, especially the photos don't belong to me. I've used two great online resources for stock photos, Fotolia and iStockphoto, because I wanted to include a variety of projects and I don't happen to photograph all of those type of subjects. For example, in Chapter 1, I think the basketball sports poster is a great way to use layers, but I don't shoot basketball, so I used stock photos. And you can guarantee that I didn't use photos of anyone I know for the retouching chapter, so I've used stock photos for many of those tutorials, as well.

2. I've included four online videos to go along with the book: one on layer basics, one on selection basics, one on brush basics, and a tutorial on the making of the cover. We use brushes and selections throughout the book, so I wanted to make sure you're up to speed with the basics of what you'll need.

3. What's new in this version of the book? For starters, I've added an entire chapter on advanced layer techniques, blending, and compositing. Overall though, layers haven't really changed much since I wrote the first version of this book more than three years ago. But Photoshop has had two major releases since then, and it was time to bring the book up to date. So, I have included all new graphics, examples, and even some new techniques that are more current for today's Photoshop user. That said, if you bought the first version of this book and you're looking for a completely new book, please don't buy this one (if you're flipping through it in a bookstore. If you've already bought it online, most online booksellers allow returns, so return it now before you feel the need to write a nasty review on Amazon.com :-).

4. Feel free to read the book in any order you want. I organized the book into the logical way that I teach layers when I teach it to a live class. I started with the easier stuff and moved on to the more advanced stuff in later chapters. So jump in wherever you want. Hey, it's your book. You bought it, right? You're smart enough to realize that if you jumped right to Chapter 6 and are lost, that the best thing to do may be to backtrack to Chapter 1. Chapter 10, however, assumes you've read the rest of the book.

5. There's a little bonus at the end of each chapter. As an author, it's one of the ways that we wreak havoc on our editors, and we take a small amount of pleasure in that. After all, you can't just fill the book with tutorials, right? You've got to throw some tips in, and throw them in at the last minute after all of the chapters are already turned in. My thoughts exactly. So, at the end of each chapter, there's a page of some common "How Do I…" questions. They're all related to things that you read in the chapter. I've taken the most common questions and put them into one place, so you don't have to poke around the whole chapter to find them.

That's it. That's my introduction. Easy. Simple. Short. Sweet. Getting longer now that I keep adding to it at the end. But, still shorter than most. Now, get to it and enjoy the book. —Matt K.

CHAPTER ONE

LAYER BASICS

This first chapter is named Layer Basics, because it's where you should go if you're brand new to layers. While I start with the basics, we'll move pretty quickly and cover some very cool things you should know. So even if you think you're somewhat familiar with layers, you'll still want to read through it. That said, if you're pretty familiar with the concept of layers and why they're important, you can skip the first tutorial and jump right to the second one—that's where things really start to take off. As for the third tutorial...well, let's just say it gets flat-out crazy. You'll be amazed at all the things that you can do with layers (and all of the little things you never knew about them) after you read it.

fx ▣ ◑ ▭ ▣

LAYER BASICS

READ THIS IF YOU'RE NOT REALLY SURE WHY YOU WOULD USE LAYERS

Let me preface this tutorial by saying it is only meant for those of you who don't really understand why you would use layers. If you already know why layers are important, then skip this tutorial and go straight to the next one, where we dive right into building things with layers. Okay, so if you're sticking around, then let's talk a little bit about layers and how they're the foundation of everything you do in Adobe Photoshop. Think of it this way: if you were to take a printed photograph, you'd never dream of drawing over it with a black marker and then expect to go back and erase that drawing, would you? Well, that's exactly what you're doing if you don't use layers in Photoshop and you work on the original image. By the way, as well as making the images used here in the book available on a website (the link is in the introduction), I've also included a video there to help you better understand what you're about to see here, so make sure you stop by and watch it.

STEP 1: IMAGINE DRAWING ON A PHOTO

Picture this: you're holding a printed photo of me. Why? Because I didn't think it was right to do what I'm about to do to a portrait of someone else. Seriously, though, it can be any printed photo. The point is, imagine you set that photo down on the desk, grabbed a black marker, and started drawing on it—fake eyeglasses, a mustache, and maybe even a funny beard.

BRAD MOORE

STEP 2: TRY TO ERASE WHAT YOU JUST DREW

BRAD MOORE

Now, what would happen if you grabbed a damp towel and tried to erase what you just drew? One of two things would most likely happen: (a) you would start to erase the drawing marks, but you'd probably start to ruin the photo under them, as well, or (b) you wouldn't be able to erase anything (if you used a permanent marker) and you'd be stuck with a pretty funny-looking photo.

STEP 3: NOW, THIS TIME WE HAVE A PIECE OF TRANSPARENT PAPER

BRAD MOORE

Let's take this example one step further. Back up to the point where you have a photo that you want to draw over. This time, though, you also have a piece of transparent paper.

STEP 4: PLACE THE TRANSPARENT PAPER OVER THE PHOTO AND DRAW

Now when you place the photo down on the desk and get ready to draw, you place the transparent piece of paper over it. Just like before, imagine taking a black marker and drawing over the photo. However, unlike before, you're not drawing directly on the photo itself—instead, you're drawing on the transparent paper. It looks the same, though, right?

BRAD MOORE

STEP 5: TRY TO ERASE WHAT YOU JUST DREW

After you see the final result, you'll probably decide that I look much better without a mustache. Once again, try erasing what you just drew with that damp cloth. Now it's a breeze. Or, if you're unhappy with the entire project, then just toss the transparent piece of paper into the garbage and start over again. By using that transparent piece of paper, you've gained a tremendous amount of flexibility.

BRAD MOORE

STEP 6: MOVE INTO PHOTOSHOP

Okay, enough imagining. I promise we'll actually be using Photoshop for the rest of the book. Go ahead and open a photo in Photoshop by clicking on the File menu and choosing Open (or just press Command-O [PC: Ctrl-O]). Navigate to the photo you want (or just use the photo of me), click on it, and click Open. Now you'll see the photo, but more importantly, notice the Layers panel. If you don't see it, just choose Window>Layers. You should notice that there's only one layer in the Layers panel—it's called Background.

TIP: You can use the keyboard shortcut F7 to hide-and-show the Layers panel, so you don't have to keep going under the Window menu to get to it.

STEP 7: DRAW ON THE BACKGROUND LAYER

Select the Brush tool from the Toolbox (or just press B) and click on the brush thumbnail on the left side of the Options Bar. Select a small, hard-edged brush from the Brush Picker. Press the letter D to set your Foreground color to black and start painting on the photo. Have at it—a funny face, glasses, a mustache, whatever you want!

STEP 8: TRY ERASING WHAT YOU JUST DREW

After you're done painting on the photo, you'll inevitably think it looked much better before the vandalism (sorry, I meant to say artwork). So, select the Eraser tool (E) from the Toolbox and try to erase those brush strokes away. See what happens? Not only do you erase away the black brush strokes, but the underlying photo is erased, as well (you see white here because my Background color is set to white). Not good, but as you can imagine, there's a better way to do this. Go ahead and close this image, but make sure you don't save the changes.

STEP 9: ADD A BLANK LAYER ON TOP OF THE ORIGINAL PHOTO

Let's bring this example back around to the photo with the transparent piece of paper. Remember how well it worked to isolate our drawing on the transparent piece of paper? Well, layers give us the same benefit. Open a new image (or use the same one of me) and click on the Create a New Layer icon at the bottom of the Layers panel (circled in red here). You'll see a new layer, named Layer 1, now appears on top of the Background layer. This new layer is just like that transparent piece of paper.

STEP 10: USE THE BRUSH TOOL TO PAINT ON THE NEW LAYER

Press B to select the Brush tool again, like you did in Step 7. Click once on Layer 1 in the Layers panel to make sure it's selected (you've got to click on a layer to select it in the Layers panel. If you don't, then you may be working on the wrong layer. Always look for the layer that is highlighted in color. That is the current or active layer and the one that you'll be editing). Then start painting on it just like before. Everything should look and act exactly the same.

STEP 11: ERASE AWAY BRUSH STROKES THAT YOU DON'T WANT

Finally, to bring this example back around full circle, select the Eraser tool again and erase away any of those brush strokes. You'll see that you can easily erase them without affecting the original photo. That's because you created your changes on a separate, blank layer on top of the photo. You never touched the original photo, just the layer on top of it.

There you have it my friends— the totally basic introduction to layers. Don't forget to stop by the website (mentioned in the introduction) to watch the video and download the images to follow along with. Now, roll your sleeves up and get ready—we've got some really cool stuff ahead.

USING MULTIPLE LAYERS

COMBINING SEVERAL IMAGES TO BUILD A MULTI-LAYERED IMAGE IS WHERE THIS STUFF GETS REALLY COOL

The main idea behind this tutorial is to use multiple images and get used to the way layer stacking works. Working with one image is great, but things get much more useful when you start bringing multiple images into one Photoshop document. There are going to be plenty of times where you want to take a layer from one image and add it into the one you're working on. A great example would be blending multiple photos together to create some type of collage.

STEP 1: OPEN SEVERAL PHOTOS THAT YOU'D LIKE TO COMBINE

First off, open the photos that you'd like to combine into one image. Click on the File menu and choose Open. Then navigate to each photo aand click Open. Here, we're going to combine three photos, so I've opened all three and can see them in my workspace.

Note: If you're a Mac user, you'll notice that I have the Application Frame turned off (Window> Application Frame) for the tutorials in this book. I've also turned off the Open Documents as Tabs interface preference (Command-K [PC: Ctrl-K]), so that my image windows don't appear tabbed.

STEP 2: CREATE A NEW DOCUMENT TO HOLD YOUR NEW IMAGE

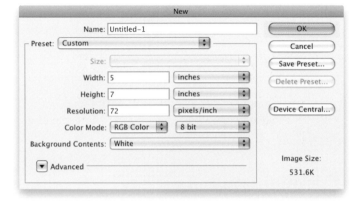

Now let's create a brand new document to hold what we're about to create. Click on the File menu and choose New. For this example, we're going to create a promo card for a basketball team. I want my new document to be 7" tall by 5" wide, so change the unit of measurement to Inches (when you change the width it'll automatically change the height, too), then enter 5 inches for Width and 7 inches for Height. Since we're just display-ing this onscreen, change the resolution to 72 ppi. If we were going to print this, we'd probably use something between 240 ppi and 300 ppi. Click OK to create the new blank document.

STEP 3: COPY-AND-PASTE ONE OF THE PHOTOS INTO THE NEW DOCUMENT

We need to get the photos into the new blank document now. There are a couple ways to do this and each have their place. First, let's try the one I use the most—copy-and-paste: Click on the photo of the half-basketball to bring it to the front and make it the active document. Click on the Select menu and choose All to select the entire image. Copy this selection by choosing Edit>Copy. Now, click over to the blank document and paste the copied photo into it by choosing Edit>Paste. By the way, we're not going to use the Edit menu for these anymore. The key-board shortcuts for Copy and Paste are Command-C (PC: Ctrl-C) and Command-V (PC: Ctrl-V), respec-tively, and they work a lot faster.

STEP 4: NOTICE THE NEW LAYER IN THE BLANK DOCUMENT

Right after you paste the image, you should see a new layer called Layer 1 appear in the Layers panel right above the Background layer. By default, Photoshop automatically creates a new layer whenever you paste something into an image. This is a good thing because it forces us to work on multiple layers. Now select the Move tool from the Toolbox (or just press V), click on the pasted image, and drag it toward the bottom of the document.

TIP: While dragging with the Move tool, you can press-and-hold the Shift key to keep the layer on the same vertical or horizontal line.

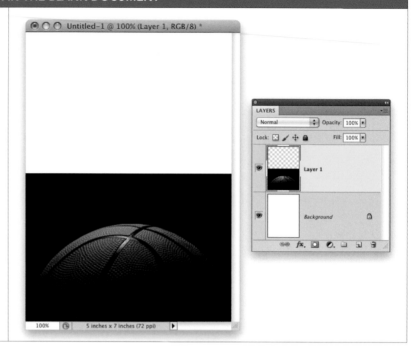

STEP 5: BRING ANOTHER PHOTO INTO THE NEW DOCUMENT

Let's bring another photo into the new document. Before, we used copy-and-paste, but there's another way: you can also click-and-drag images into other documents. Position the new document window and the photo of the basketball player so you can see both next to each other. Click once on the player photo to make it the active document, and with the Move tool, click on the player photo, and drag it over into the new document (that's why you need to be able to see both of them). Once your cursor is over the new document, release the mouse button and your photo will appear as a new layer. Use the Move tool to center it in the document.

STEP 6: MOVE THE THIRD PHOTO INTO THE NEW DOCUMENT

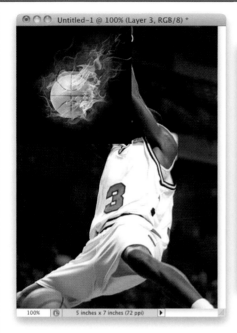

Go ahead and bring the last photo (the basketball photo with the flames) into the new document. I recommend the copy-and-paste method, since it's easier for me, but feel free to use whichever way works best for you. Once it's there, use the Move tool to move it to the top left of the image.

STEP 7: REARRANGE THE LAYERS IN YOUR NEW DOCUMENT

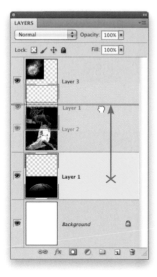
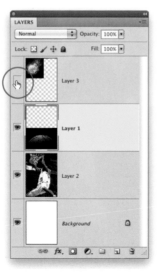

Close the original three photos. We don't need them open anymore because we've copied their contents into layers in our new document. (The layers in our new image are not connected to their originals. No matter what you do here, you won't affect the originals.) Now, notice how the basketball player on Layer 2 totally hides the basketball on Layer 1? That's because Layer 2 is on top of Layer 1. Let's swap them by clicking on Layer 1 in the Layers panel and dragging it above Layer 2. Now, you'll see the contents of Layer 1 on top of Layer 2. One more thing: we're going to work on Layer 3 last, so let's hide it by clicking the little Eye icon to the left of the layer's thumbnail in the Layers panel (circled here in red).

STEP 8: SELECT THE ERASER TOOL AND CHANGE THE SETTINGS

Now, we're going to blend these layers together, so select the Eraser tool from the Toolbox (or just press E). In the Options Bar, click on the brush thumbnail to open the Brush Picker, and set the Size to something large (like 250 pixels) and the Hardness to 0% to create a large, soft-edged brush. Also, set the Opacity to 30%. By using a lower opacity setting, we'll be able to lightly erase away parts of the photos that are on top of each other and give the illusion that they're blending together, since you'll see whatever is below them. If we used a 100% setting, you'd see some obvious seams and erase marks. The lower opacity will allow us to blend things better.

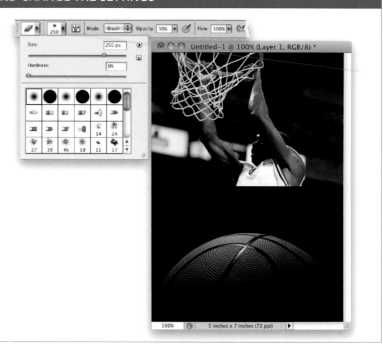

STEP 9: USE THE ERASER TOOL TO BLEND THE PHOTOS

With Layer 1 (the half-basketball) active in the Layers panel, start erasing away the left, top, and right part of the black background of the photo—just a few clicks with the Eraser tool should do it. Remember, though, you're working with a tool that's set to one-third strength (the Opacity setting), so you're only erasing a little bit at a time. The more times you click, the more you'll erase. So, just keep erasing and you'll reveal the contents of Layer 2 (the basketball player), which is below it in the layer stack (press the Left Bracket key to decrease the size of your brush as you get closer to the basketball). This makes the two photos blend together.

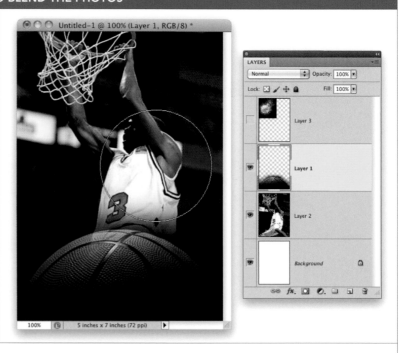

STEP 10: BLEND THE LAST PHOTO

Go back and make the image on Layer 3 visible again (click in the little box where the Eye icon used to be to the left of the layer's thumbnail) and do the same thing to the basketball with flames that we just did in Step 9 (be sure to click on Layer 3 in the Layers panel first to make it active). Make your brush size smaller and erase away the black area around the basketball, along with some of the flames, so only the basketball shows over the net and not its black background. Since it's on top of Layer 2 in the layer stack, wherever you erase, you'll be revealing the photo on that layer. Again, this blends them together making it look like the photos were smoothly merged together.

STEP 11: OPEN A LOGO IMAGE

Finally, let's bring in a finishing logo. Open the image that has the graphics and logo that you want to add. So far, we've been opening JPEG images and dragging them in, but you can just as easily open other types of files, too, including Photoshop PSD files. Here, I've got a PSD file that has a logo on its own layer.

STEP 12: MOVE THE LOGO INTO YOUR IMAGE TO FINISH THINGS UP

Go back to your new image and make sure the top layer in your Layers panel (Layer 3) is active (this is important, because when you bring the logo over to this document, it will appear above whichever layer is active in your Layers panel. Save time by clicking on the layer you want it to appear above). Now, click-and-drag (or copy-and-paste) the logo from the other image. It'll appear at the very top of the layer stack, ready to be positioned where you need it.

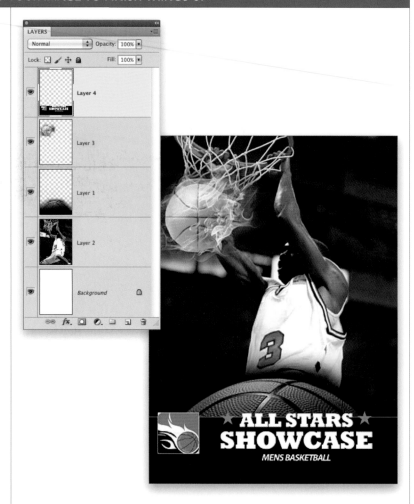

EVERYTHING ELSE ABOUT LAYERS

THERE'S A TON OF FEATURES, TIPS, AND TRICKS IN THE LAYERS PANEL TO HELP YOU WORK BETTER

If there is one tutorial in this book not to skip, it's this one. Even if you think you know layers pretty well up to this point, this tutorial will show you more. Trust me. See, we're going to build a project. It's a big project, I know. But along the way, we're going to see all the things in the Layers panel that help you work better. We'll look at moving multiple layers at the same time, linking layers, resizing layers, aligning layers, merging and flattening, and even which features in the Layers panel are worth using and which ones actually hold you up. We'll even see how to get around that dreaded locked Background layer so you can actually do something with it. So don't skip this tutorial. By the time you get done with it, you will be a layers pro and the rest of what you read in this book will be a breeze.

STEP 1: OPEN THE IMAGE THAT WILL BE YOUR BACKGROUND

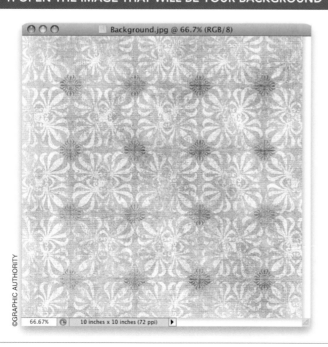

In this tutorial, we're going to create a wedding album page. Start by opening the main image that will be the background of the page (File>Open). Here, I'm using a textured background that I got from Graphic Authority's "Behind the Scenes-Patterns" collection (www.graphicauthority.com).

TIP: If you're ever looking for backgrounds or other elements to build album pages, I always point people to Graphic Authority for complete sets (or other websites like www.fotolia.com or www.istockphoto.com). Paying a few bucks for a quick background sure beats taking the time to make them from scratch.

STEP 2: HOW TO MAKE YOUR LAYERS PANEL THUMBNAILS LARGER

Before we move on, I've got to share this tip with you. You're seriously going to love me for this one. Ever thought the thumbnails in the Layers panel were too small? Well, you can change them. Every panel has a flyout menu associated with it, and the Layers panel is no different. Click on the little icon with the down-facing arrow and four lines next to it at the top right of the panel. Choose Palette Options from this flyout menu, select the largest thumbnail option by clicking on its radio button in the dialog, and then click OK. Now sit back and revel in the seemingly inhuman-sized Layers panel thumbnails.

STEP 3: MAKE YOUR BACKGROUND LAYER A REGULAR LAYER

Notice how the name of the bottom layer in the Layers panel is always "Background"? If you haven't already, you will undoubtedly come to hate that Background layer because you simply can't do certain things to it. You can't move it with the Move tool and you can't change its position in the layer stacking order, either. Well I'm here to tell you that you can change all that. Make the Background layer a regular layer by just double-clicking on the word Background and clicking OK in the New Layer dialog. Now it's a regular layer. Sweet, huh?

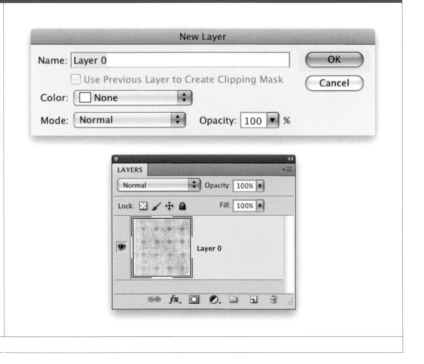

STEP 4: CREATE A NEW LAYER BELOW THE BACKGROUND

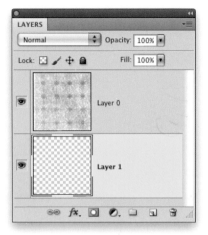

Next, we're going to spice up the background texture a little by adding some depth to it. Since the texture layer isn't the Background layer anymore, we can actually add a layer below it. You could always click on the Create a New Layer icon at the bottom of the panel to create a new layer on top of the texture layer and then click-and-drag it beneath it, but there's a shortcut: press-and-hold the Command (PC: Ctrl) key and click on the Create a New Layer icon, and the new layer will automatically be added below the currently selected layer.

STEP 5: ADD A GRADIENT TO THE NEW BLANK LAYER

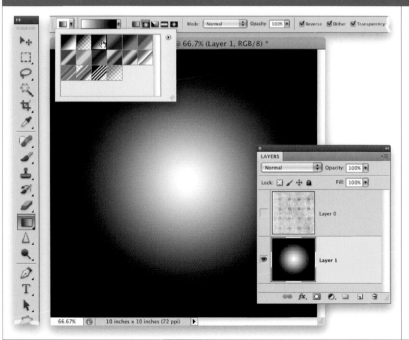

Click on the small Eye icon to the left of the texture layer's thumbnail to hide that layer and, with the new blank layer you just added at the bottom active, add a white-to-black radial gradient. To do this, select the Gradient tool from the Toolbox (G), click on the down-facing arrow to the right of the gradient thumbnail in the Options Bar, and choose the Black, White gradient from the Gradient Picker. Now, click on the Radial Gradient icon (it's the second icon to the right of the gradient thumbnail), turn on the Reverse checkbox (also in the Options Bar), then starting in the middle of your document, just drag from left to right to add a gradient to the bottom layer.

STEP 6: MAKE THE TEXTURE LAYER VISIBLE AGAIN AND REDUCE ITS OPACITY

Next, we're going to use the gradient to give our background texture some depth and dimension. Click on the box to the left of the texture layer's thumbnail to make it visible again. We just added a gradient, but we don't see it anymore because the texture layer now hides it. The Opacity setting, though, will let us blend the two together. So, click on the top texture layer to make it active. Move your cursor over the word "Opacity" in the top right of the Layers panel. You'll see two little arrows appear on either side of the hand cursor. If you click-and-drag your cursor to the left, you'll decrease the Opacity setting, allowing you to see through the texture to the gradient below. Here, I set the Opacity to 85%.

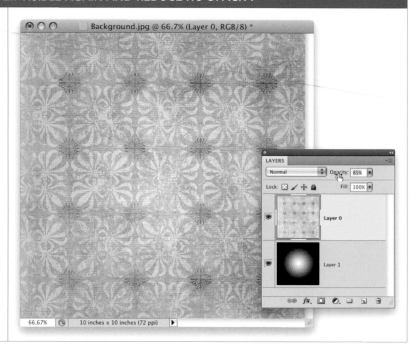

STEP 7: OPEN THE PHOTOS THAT WILL GO ON THE ALBUM PAGE AND DRAG THE FIRST ONE IN

Open the photos that are going to be included on the album page. Here, I'm going to use three photos of a couple on their wedding day. Let's start with the photo of the bride alone. With the Move tool (V), click on the photo, then drag it into your album image, and place it toward the left. As you can see, it happens to pretty much fit right in and is a good size for what we're looking for. That's not always the case, though, so read on to the next step.

©ISTOCKPHOTO/MARCO ONOFRI

STEP 8: PASTE A PORTION OF A PHOTO INTO THE ALBUM LAYOUT

Let's move on to the next photo. I know that I want two small square photos toward the right of this layout, and just by looking at this image of the bride in the car window, you can tell it's not going to work, because it's not square. So, instead of bringing the entire photo in, let's just take a selection. Grab the Rectangular Marquee tool (M). Press-and-hold the Shift key (which keeps your selection square) and make a square selection over the area you want. Now press Command-C (PC: Ctrl-C) to Copy and then Command-V (PC: Ctrl-V) to Paste that selected area into the album layout. You'll see only the selected part of the photo is placed and it's on its own layer.

STEP 9: RESIZE THE PHOTO

We got lucky with the first photo of the bride—it was the exact size we wanted. I'll be the first to tell you that it will never happen again. More often than not, you'll have to resize the images you add. In this case, the photo of the bride in the car window is still too big. The best way to resize precisely is to choose Edit>Transform>Scale, and enter the exact Width and Height settings you want up in the Options Bar. In this case, enter 188 px for the Width setting and 188 px for the Height setting. Don't forget to actually type the "px" after 188 (for pixels) or bad things will happen. Press Return (PC: Enter) when you're done.

STEP 10: PASTE AND RESIZE THE REMAINING PHOTO

Now we need to bring the third photo into the wedding album image. Make a selection of only the part of the photo where you can see the couple kissing. Press Command-C to Copy and then Command-V to Paste the selection into the wedding album image. Resize it just like in the previous step, so it's exactly 188×188 pixels in size. Finally, use the Move tool to position it somewhere below the other one (no need to be exact, because we'll take care of aligning them in the next step).

STEP 11: SELECT TWO LAYERS AT ONCE, SO WE CAN ALIGN THE PHOTOS PRECISELY

As you can see, the two small photos we just added to the album image probably aren't perfectly aligned. We could try to precisely align each one of them with the Move tool, but it's way too hard to really be exact when you're just eyeballing it. Instead, let's use Photoshop's Align Layers options. First, we need to select the layers we want to align in the Layers panel. Click on one of the photo layers in the Layers panel and then Command-click (PC: Ctrl-click) on the other layer to select multiple layers. You'll be able to tell that both are selected because they'll be highlighted with a color (the layers not selected will not be highlighted).

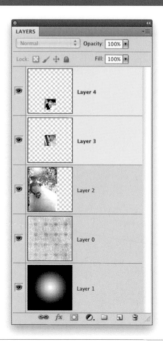

STEP 12: ALIGN THE TWO PHOTO LAYERS TO THE RIGHT

Now you need to tell Photoshop where to align the layers. First, choose Select>All (or press Command-A [PC: Ctrl-A]) to select the whole canvas, so Photoshop sees a selection edge around the entire album image. Then, from the Layer menu, choose Align Layers To Selection>Right Edges. This pushes all of the photos up against the right edge of the album image. It's automatic, so there's no manual effort required on your part.

STEP 13: REPOSITION BOTH PHOTOS TOGETHER

Remember how you selected the two photo layers back in Step 11? Let's say you decide you want to move those two smaller photos somewhere else in the album image. Since they're both still selected, there's a temporary link between the two layers and any moves you make will affect both at the same time. Press Command-D (PC: Ctrl-D) to remove your selection from the entire image, and then, using the Move tool, click-and-drag one of the photos toward the left, so it's not right up against the right edge of the image (I like this placement better actually). The other photo will follow right along. When you're done, just click on one of the layers in the Layers panel to deselect the other.

STEP 14: CREATING A PERMANENT LINK

If you want to create a more permanent connection between the two layers, so that every time you move one of them, the other follows, Photoshop lets you create a link between them that lasts even after you click on another layer to do something else. To create this link, select both of the smaller photo layers, just like we did before. Then click on the Link Layers icon at the bottom of the Layers panel (the first icon on the left, circled here in red). Now, click on one of the layers, so that only one is active, then use the Move tool and move one photo, and both of them will move together. With this permanent link, from now on, you'll only have to select one layer to move and the other(s) will follow.

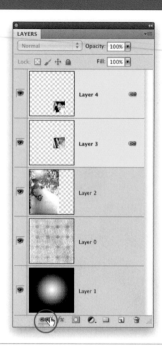

STEP 15: RENAME YOUR LAYERS TO HELP KEEP TRACK OF THINGS

Let's take a break from copying, pasting, and moving for a minute. As your Layers panel starts growing, you should name your layers to keep things organized. Click on the arrow at the top right of the Layers panel and choose Layer Properties from the flyout menu. In the resulting dialog, you'll see a Name field and a Color pop-up menu. But I've got to tell ya—that's the lame way to do it. No one uses color-coded layers, so forget this option even exists. There's a much easier way to rename a layer. Just double-click on the layer name in the Layers panel, the name will highlight, and you can then type a new name (as seen here for the three photo layers).

STEP 16: ADD A STROKE AROUND THE FIRST SMALL PHOTO

Now, back to our album page. Let's add a white stroke around the small photos. Click on the Bride in Car layer to make it the active layer, then press-and-hold the Command (PC: Ctrl) key and click on the layer's thumbnail. This puts a selection around whatever is on that layer. Click on the Create a New Layer icon at the bottom of the panel to create a new layer on top of this layer. From the Edit menu, choose Stroke. Set the Width to 3 px, the Color to white (click on the swatch), the Location to Inside, and click OK. Press Command-D to Deselect and you'll see a white stroke around the photo. Go ahead and rename this stroke layer something more descriptive, too.

STEP 17: DUPLICATE THE STROKE AND ADD IT TO THE OTHER SMALL PHOTO

I've got a killer keyboard short-cut for you here: Let's duplicate the stroke layer, so we can add it around the other small photo. If you click on the arrow at the top right of the Layers panel, you'll see there's a Duplicate Layer option in the panel's flyout menu—there is also a shortcut, though. If you press Command-J (PC: Ctrl-J), it duplicates whatever you have selected on a layer. If you have nothing selected, then it'll dupli-cate the entire contents of the layer. Trust me, you'll use this over and over again, because it's easy and saves a ton of time. So, go ahead and press Command-J to duplicate the stroke layer and then move this stroke layer copy so it appears on top of the other small photo in the Layers panel.

STEP 18: TIDY YOUR LAYERS PANEL UP BY GROUPING

Another housekeeping idea for the Layers panel is to group your layers into folders (a.k.a. Groups). Let's do this for the two small photos and their associated stroke layers. Click on the first layer to select it and then Shift-click on the last layer to select them all. From the Layer menu, choose Group Layers. This puts all of those layers into a little folder in the Layers panel. You can click the right-facing arrow at the left of the Group 1 layer to open and close the group so you can see and hide the layers in it. You can also click on the Group 1 layer and use the Move tool to move all of the layers in the group at the same time.

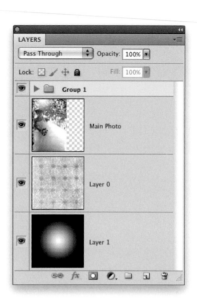

STEP 19: CREATE A RECTANGULAR SELECTION OVER THE BACKGROUND TEXTURE

Next, let's add some simple colored rectangles to the background. Click on the background texture layer in the Layers panel to make it the active layer, then click on the Create a New Layer icon at the bottom of the panel to add a new layer above the background texture, but below the large photo of the bride. Using the Rectangular Marquee tool, make a tall, thin selection to the right of the main bride photo. Click on the Foreground Color swatch at the bottom of the Toolbox to open the Color Picker and set the color to R: 137, G: 160, B: 165. Click OK to close the Color Picker.

STEP 20: FILL THE RECTANGLE WITH THE FOREGROUND COLOR AND REDUCE THE OPACITY

Now, press Option-Delete (PC: Alt-Backspace) to fill that selection with the Foreground color. Since the color appears a little obtrusive as it is, let's make it a bit more subtle. At the top of the Layers panel, reduce the Opacity setting of this layer to 50% (we did this earlier in the project with the texture background for the gradient layer we added below it). Press Command-D (PC: Ctrl-D) to Deselect.

STEP 21: CREATE ANOTHER RECTANGLE

Click on the Create a New Layer icon again to add one more new layer on top of the current rectangle layer. Then, create another thin rectangular selection (thinner than the first one and to its left) with the Rectangular Marquee tool. Press D, then X to set your Foreground color to white, and press Option-Delete to fill that selection with white. Deselect, and now you've got some extra color and a nice way to separate that large photo from the background.

STEP 22: CLEAN UP BY DELETING UNNECESSARY LAYERS

Another task to do often is delete any layers that aren't needed or that you just don't like. For example, let's say you don't like the teal rectangle you added a few steps back. You could click on the little Eye icon to the left of the layer thumbnail to turn it off, but that still leaves the layer. To delete it permanently, click on that layer and drag it onto the Trash icon at the bottom of the Layers panel. Once you know you want something removed, deleting layers is a good habit to get into as you're working because it helps keep file size to a minimum and Photoshop running faster overall. Plus, it cuts down on clutter in the Layers panel. I kinda like it with the teal rectangle, so I'm not going to delete it, but I wanted to show you how it's done.

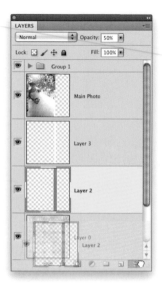

STEP 23: ADD TEXT TO FINISH THINGS OFF

We're almost done. One of the last things we need to do is add the date of the wedding to the album layout. (We'll get into creating Type layers in Chapter 5, so for this project, I've just provided a PSD file that has the text in it.) Open the type file and copy-and-paste the Date layer into the album layout (move the Date layer to the top of the layer stack in the Layers panel, if you want it to appear over any of the images). It'll look cool if it's turned sideways, so go to Edit>Transform>Rotate 90 CCW. This will automatically rotate the date, so it reads bottom to top. Using the Move tool, drag it toward the top-right corner of the layout.

Finally, I'd merge any layers that don't need to stay editable. You see, every layer you have in the Layers panel takes up space in your file and your computer's memory. Plus, too many layers are just plain hard to deal with. Who wants an image with 20, 30, or even more layers in it? So I merge (flatten) layers often when I know I don't need to change something. A great example here would be the small square photos and their stroke layers (which we placed in a group in Step 18). To merge them, select both layers first (as seen here). Then from the Layers panel's flyout menu, choose Merge Layers. This squishes both layers into one. You won't be able to edit the stroke independently of the photo it was around anymore, but you probably don't care at this point. That's it! The über layers project is complete. The only thing left to do is save the image as a PSD file (choose File>Save As), so you can reopen it later and still edit all of the layers if you need to.

HOW DO I...

CREATE A NEW LAYER?

Press Command-Shift-N (PC: Ctrl-Shift-N) or click on the Create a New Layer icon at the bottom of the Layers panel.

CREATE A NEW LAYER WITHOUT SEEING THE NEW LAYER DIALOG?

Press Command-Option-Shift-N (PC: Ctrl-Alt-Shift-N) or click on the Create a New Layer icon at the bottom of the Layers panel.

RENAME A LAYER?

Double-click on the name of the layer in the Layers panel and type a new name.

CONVERT A BACKGROUND LAYER TO A REGULAR LAYER?

Double-click on the Background layer in the Layers panel. Then click OK in the New Layer dialog to accept the new name. Or, even better, you can press-and-hold the Option (PC: Alt) key and double-click on the Background layer in the Layers panel, and that bypasses the New Layer dialog.

DUPLICATE A LAYER?

Press Command-J (PC: Ctrl-J) or click-and-drag the layer onto the Create a New Layer icon at the bottom of the Layers panel.

MOVE A LAYER UP OR DOWN IN THE LAYER STACK?

There are two ways actually. The first is with the mouse: just click-and-drag a layer up or down in the layer stack. You can also do it with keyboard shortcuts: To move a layer up in the stack, press Command-] (Right Bracket key; PC: Ctrl-]). To move a layer down in the layer stack, press Command-[(Left Bracket key; PC: Ctrl-[).

SELECT MULTIPLE LAYERS AT ONCE?

Click on one layer, then press-and-hold the Command (PC: Ctrl) key, and click on any other layers you want to select. If they are contiguous, click on the first layer and then Shift-click on the last layer to select them all.

GROUP LAYERS INTO A FOLDER?

Select the layers you want to group. Then press Command-G (PC: Ctrl-G).

CHAPTER TWO

BLENDING LAYERS

Blending layers is the next level of merging your images together. There are a lot of ways to blend layers together that go beyond simply changing the opacity. One of those ways is called blend modes. It's like opacity on steroids, and the effects you can get with blend modes are unlike any other effects you'll find in Photoshop. That said, I gotta tell ya, there are a lot of blend modes in Photoshop. My goal in this chapter is to show you only those you really need to know about. Most of the blend modes will probably never get used, so we're just going to concentrate on the ones that you're going to use often. In fact, turn the page and you'll see the first tutorial is named "The Three Blend Modes You Need Most."

THE THREE BLEND MODES YOU NEED MOST

START HERE FOR A QUICK INTRODUCTION TO BLEND MODES AND WHICH THREE BLEND MODES YOU NEED MOST

I mentioned in the introduction to this chapter that there are a lot of blend modes—27 in the Layers panel, to be exact, plus a few more hidden in some other places in Photoshop. If you had to know what all of them did, you'd probably never get anything done (not to mention you'd be a geek and all of your friends would make fun of you). That's where this tutorial comes in. Forget about the 27 blend modes and concentrate on just the three you need most.

STEP 1: OPEN A PHOTO TO EXPERIMENT WITH

Start off by opening a photo to experiment with. It can be a photo of anything at this point. It doesn't matter. We just need an image to work with. (Remember, if you want to follow along using my images, you can download them at the website I listed in the introduction.) We're going to do things a little differently in this tutorial. I'm going to go through two examples for each of the three blend modes you'll use the most to help you see what is going on. The first will be a not-so-real-world example of a blend mode and the second will be a real-world use of the same blend mode. I think you'll see that each example helps you understand what's going on with blend modes in its own way.

MATT KLOSKOWSKI

STEP 2: ADD A NEW LAYER AND SELECT THE GRADIENT TOOL

Okay, we need to set up our not-so-real-world example of blend modes. Create a new layer above the Background layer by clicking on the Create a New Layer icon at the bottom of the Layers panel. Then, select the Gradient tool (G) from the Toolbox. Press Return (PC: Enter) to bring up the Gradient Picker. It'll show up wherever your cursor is on the screen. Choose the third gradient from the left in the top row. It's one of the default gradients called Black, White. Press Esc to close the Gradient Picker. Finally, make sure you select Linear Gradient in the Options Bar (it's the first icon to the right of the gradient thumbnail).

STEP 3: APPLY A LINEAR GRADIENT ACROSS THE IMAGE

Click once in the Layers panel on the new layer you created in Step 2. Then, with the Gradient tool selected, click-and-drag on your image from the far left across to the far right to put a black-to-white linear gradient on that layer. This is the layer we're going to use to see what's really going on behind the scenes of the three blend modes we'll be looking at.

STEP 4: CHOOSE BLEND MODE #1—MULTIPLY

Let's look at the first really useful blend mode. It's called Multiply. With the gradient layer you just created in Step 3 still selected, click on the blend mode pop-up menu in the top-left corner of the Layers panel, and choose Multiply. So, what just happened? Well, where changing the layer's Opacity setting changes the opacity of *everything* on a layer, changing a layer blend mode changes the opacity of things differently depending on their colors.

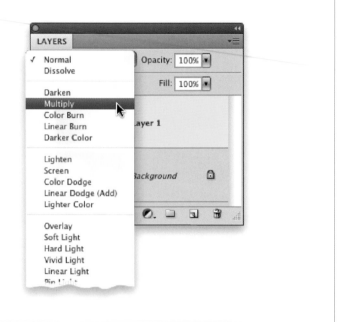

STEP 5: BLEND MODE #1—MULTIPLY (A NOT-SO-REAL-WORLD EXAMPLE)

Multiply, for example, always has the effect of darkening, except where things are white. Think of it this way: Multiply multiplies two colors (the top layer times the layer under it). Black times any color will result in black, as you can see from the far left of the image. Gray multiplied with any color results in something darker than the original, as you can see from the middle portion of the image. Finally, white times anything leaves it unchanged and therefore makes any white drop out or become transparent. You can see this on the right side of the image where the gradient used to be all white.

STEP 6: BLEND MODE #1—MULTIPLY (A REAL WORLD EXAMPLE)

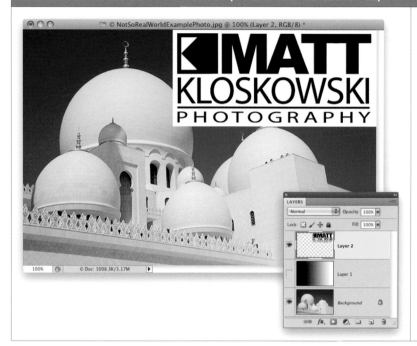

Go ahead and keep the same image open, but hide the gradient layer for a minute by clicking on the Eye icon to the left of the layer thumbnail. Now, open an image with a black logo and a white background (I provided one in the practice files, in case you want to follow along). Make sure you can see both images (if you're using tabbed documents, you'll want to go to the Window menu, under Arrange, and choose Float All in Windows). Get the Move tool (V) and click-and-drag the logo image into the same document as the photo, so the logo appears on a layer on top of the photo.

STEP 7: BLEND MODE #1—MULTIPLY (A REAL WORLD EXAMPLE)

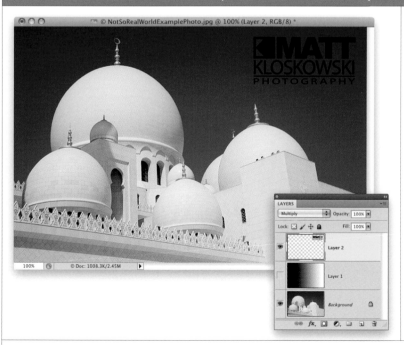

If you need to resize the logo, press Command-T (PC: Ctrl-T) to enter Free Transform, press-and-hold the Shift key to keep things proportional, grab a corner handle and drag inward. Press Return (PC: Enter) to lock in your change. Change the blend mode of the logo layer to Multiply. This is a great example of how blend modes can save you a bunch of time when you're working with simple graphics. Normally you'd think you have to select the white areas and delete them, but it's a lot easier than that. If you recall from the gradient example, the Multiply blend mode drops out all of the white and makes it transparent. Now you're only left with the parts of the logo that are black.

STEP 8: CHOOSE BLEND MODE #2—SCREEN

Now let's switch back to the gradient example. Drag the black-and-white logo layer onto the Trash icon at the bottom of the Layers panel to delete it, if you were following along, and click on the box next to the gradient layer's thumbnail to unhide it. This time, change the blend mode of the gradient layer to Screen. You'll notice it looks quite a bit different from Multiply.

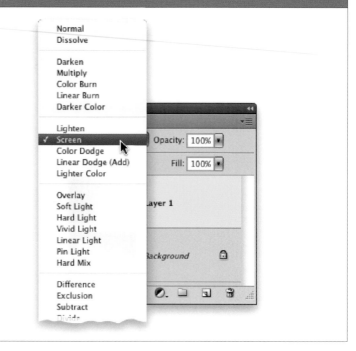

STEP 9: BLEND MODE #2—SCREEN (A NOT-SO-REAL-WORLD EXAMPLE)

Screen is considered the opposite of Multiply. I mentioned earlier that Multiply will always have the effect of making the resulting image darker. Screen, on the other hand, will always have the effect of making things lighter. It's actually the exact opposite of Multiply. Pure white will always look white—it stays the same. Gray will become lighter, depending on how dark the gray was in the first place, as you can see by the gradient. Anything that is totally black becomes transparent and gets dropped out totally.

STEP 10: BLEND MODE #2—SCREEN (A REAL WORLD EXAMPLE)

Open two images. Here I have an image of some scribbles on a black background and a photo of a child. A popular effect I've seen on family and children's portraits is to place tiny scribbles throughout the photo. So, use the Rectangular Marquee tool (M) to select a letter from the scribbles image, press Command-C (PC: Ctrl-C) to Copy the letter, switch to the photo of the little girl, and then press Command-V (PC: Ctrl-V) to Paste the letter onto it. You can use the Move tool to move it around in the photo and Free Transform to resize or rotate it.

STEP 11: BLEND MODE #2—SCREEN (A REAL WORLD EXAMPLE)

Change the blend mode of the layer with the letter G on it to Screen. As you can see, this drops out everything that was black in the image so now you're just left with a white scribble graphic. Go back and repeat the process for the rest of her name. Each time you paste a new letter, change its blend mode to Screen and when you're done, you'll have a creative way to enhance family portraits. I've also copied a few of the other scribbles and placed them throughout the photo for an added special touch.

STEP 12: CHOOSE BLEND MODE #3—SOFT LIGHT

The last of the three most important blend modes is Soft Light. Go back to the gradient example and switch the gradient layer's blend mode to Soft Light. As you can see, Soft Light has yet another totally different effect than the previous two.

TIP: Truthfully, the Overlay blend mode ranks right up there as a contender for the third most popular blend mode. It has a similar effect (but slightly stronger) to Soft Light, though, so give it a try.

STEP 13: BLEND MODE #3—SOFT LIGHT (A NOT-SO-REAL-WORLD EXAMPLE)

If you look where the gradient was black, you'll see the underlying image was darkened. Wherever the gradient was white, the underlying image was lightened. So basically, the darks were made darker and the lights were made lighter. However, anything that was 50% gray became transparent. So any areas in the center of the gradient dropped out just like white and black did for the other two examples (Multiply and Screen). This is all really another way of saying the contrast was increased. That's why Soft Light is known as a contrast-enhancing blend mode.

STEP 14: BLEND MODE #3—SOFT LIGHT (A REAL WORLD EXAMPLE)

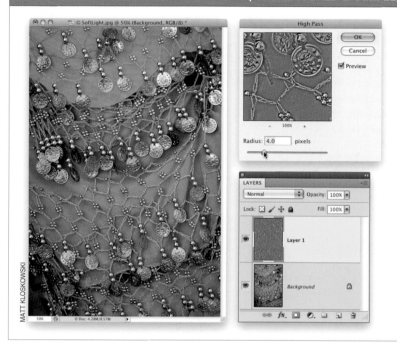

MATT KLOSKOWSKI

Open a photo with lots of small details in it that can use some sharpening. Duplicate the Background layer by pressing Command-J (PC: Ctrl-J). Go to the Filter menu and choose Other> High Pass. Enter a fairly low setting like 4 pixels (just enough so you can start to see some of the details in the gray area of the layer, but not so much they start to glow in the preview). Click OK when you're done. Notice what the High Pass filter did? It made most of the layer gray (50% gray, actually). However, it took any of the detailed areas and made them lighter or darker depending on their original color.

STEP 15: BLEND MODE #3—SOFT LIGHT (A REAL WORLD EXAMPLE)

Now change the blend mode of the High Pass layer you just created to Soft Light. Cool, huh? This has the effect of sharpening the photo by adding contrast to the edges (which is what sharpening really does). It's the same as the gradient example: Anything that was dark was made darker. Anything that was lighter in color was made even lighter. Then, just like the gradient, anything that was exactly 50% gray was made transparent and not visible in the final image. We're able to hide the gray and just get the contrast-enhancing effect of the Soft Light blend mode. Don't forget, the Overlay blend mode is just as good (if not better) in some cases, so give it a try.

A CLOSER LOOK AT BLEND MODES

LET'S TAKE A CLOSER LOOK AT THE LAYER BLEND MODES AND CREATE A COOL IMAGE, TOO

In the first tutorial of this chapter, you saw the three blend modes that you'll probably use the most. That doesn't mean the other blend modes aren't useful, though. There are lots of things you can do when you combine those three blend modes with some of the others.

STEP 1: OPEN THE PHOTOS THAT YOU'D LIKE TO BLEND TOGETHER

Open the photos that you'd like to combine. We're not going to create a collage here (we will in Chapter 4, though), so when I say blend I mean it in a different way. We're going to duplicate parts of each layer and use them to blend into each other and the layers below, using blend modes. Some will be the blend modes we've already looked at, but we'll also take a look at some other useful ones.

Note: You can go straight to Step 5 and open the PSD file I've provided if you want to skip copying-and-pasting the photos into the main document.

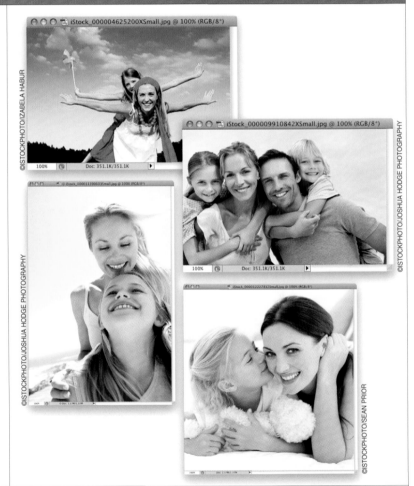

STEP 2: CREATE A BLANK DOCUMENT TO HOLD OUR NEW IMAGE

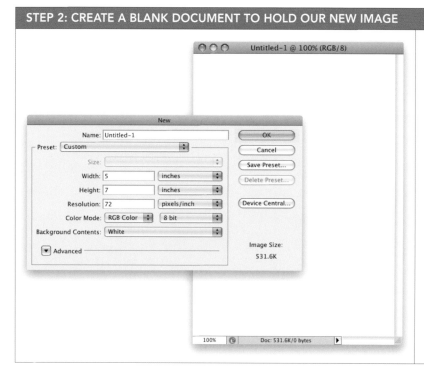

Next, press Command-N (PC: Ctrl-N) to open the New dialog. Set the Width to 5 inches and the Height to 7 inches. Then, set the Resolution to 72 ppi, the Color Mode to RGB Color, and the Background Contents to White, and click OK to create the new document.

STEP 3: BRING THE PHOTOS INTO THE NEW IMAGE. ALIGN THEM. RESIZE THEM IF NEEDED

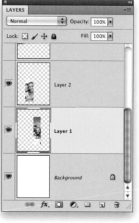

Using the Rectangular Marquee tool (M), make a selection from each photo (preferably a portion with the faces), choose Edit>Copy, switch to your new document, and choose Edit>Paste. I selected thin rectangular portions and spread them evenly across the image. One thing that'll really help you align the layers visually as you're dragging them is the View>Snap option. If it's turned on, your layers will snap to each other as you move them.

TIP: If you're not happy with the way the photos fit, choose Edit>Free Transform, or press Command-T (PC: Ctrl-T), to resize them. Press-and-hold the Shift key to constrain the aspect ratio while you're resizing.

STEP 4: MERGE YOUR LAYERS USING ONE OF THE COOLEST LAYER KEYBOARD SHORTCUTS

Once you get all of your layers into the new document, go ahead and merge them together to make them easier to work with. You could go to Layer>Flatten Image, but that would flatten them for good. Instead, we're going to use one of the coolest keyboard shortcuts in Photoshop to flatten them into one new merged layer, while keeping all of the originals separate. So, click on the top layer to make it active, then press Command-Option-Shift-E (PC: Ctrl-Alt-Shift-E). This takes every layer and flattens them together into a new layer at the top of the Layers panel. But if you look, the other layers are still there, in case you ever needed to go back and work with them.

STEP 5: LET'S TAKE A LOOK AT THE BLEND MODES BEFORE WE MOVE ON

Let's take a quick look at the layer blend mode pop-up menu. It's a long list, but there is an order in the way it's organized. Each section in the menu can be categorized: The second section from the top (1) lists the blend modes that have a darkening effect. The next section (2) lists blend modes that have a lightening effect. After that (3) are blend modes that enhance contrast. These blend modes will lighten or darken depending on the color, where the other two sections will always darken or always lighten. Section 4 (probably the least used) lists blend modes that show differences between two layers. Finally, the bottom section (5) lists blend modes that work with color.

STEP 6: DARKENING BLEND MODES—SELECT A PORTION OF THE IMAGE. COPY TO ITS OWN LAYER

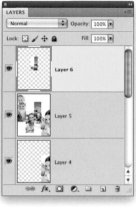

Let's start creating our blend mode design here by experimenting with the darkening blend modes. Click on the merged layer at the top of the Layers panel to select it. Get the Rectangular Marquee tool again, and make a rectangular selection that extends over two photos. Don't worry if it extends off onto the background. Duplicate that selection by pressing Command-J (PC: Ctrl-J) to put that part of the layer on its own layer.

STEP 7: CHANGE THE BLEND MODE TO COLOR BURN

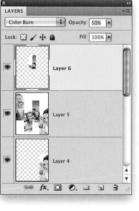

Change the blend mode of the new layer to Color Burn. Notice how it not only gets darker but appears red, too? Any blend mode that has the word "burn" in it will have just that effect. It'll make the image appear burned. This effect is a little too much for this image, so reduce the Opacity of that layer to 50% to blend it with the photo below.

Just like you did in Step 6, click on the merged layer to select it. Then make a rectangular selection around another portion of the merged image. Press Command-J to copy it onto its own layer.

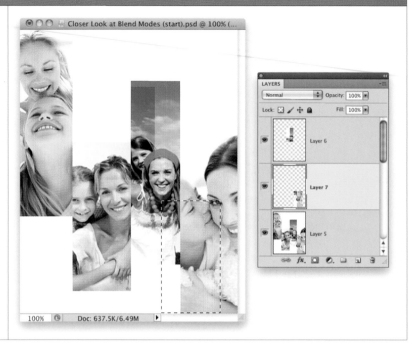

STEP 9: CHANGE THE LAYER BLEND MODE TO COLOR DODGE

Change this new layer's blend mode to one of the lightening blend modes, like Color Dodge. You already saw what Screen does in the last tutorial. Color Dodge, however, has an extreme brightening effect that's more visible than Screen. In fact, any blend mode that has the word "Dodge" in it tends to take any colors that were close to white and really blow them out, so they appear much brighter than they originally were. Reduce the effect of the Color Dodge layer by changing the layer's Opacity to 55%.

STEP 10: CONTRAST BLEND MODES—SELECT AND COPY ANOTHER PORTION OF THE IMAGE

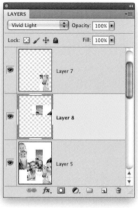

Click on the merged layer again, select another portion of the photo with the Rectangular Marquee tool, and duplicate it on its own layer. This time, change the blend mode to one of the contrast enhancing modes, like Vivid Light. All of these blend modes have the effect of making the dark colors darker and the light colors lighter, but some of them (like Vivid Light) do it in a more intense way. You'll see that Vivid Light not only makes things more contrasty, but it also makes the colors look more, well, vivid.

STEP 11: CREATE A NEW LAYER AND FILL IT WITH A SOLID COLOR

Now, let's experiment with the color-related blend modes. All of them work with the color of the layer, but the Color mode is one of the most used. First, create a new blank layer, then create a rectangular selection and fill it with a color (Edit>Fill, and choose Color from the Use pop-up menu). Any color will do, but if you want to follow what I did here, use R: 123, G: 87, B: 31. Then press Command-D (PC: Ctrl-D) to Deselect. Change the blend mode of the layer to Color. The Color blend mode turns whatever it appears over the color of the top layer. However, it has to interact with a color to work, so if it appears over white (the background here) or black, it will appear transparent.

You can repeat the previous steps a few times to see how other modes interact with the layers. Luminosity and Hue are worth trying out. Luminosity generally removes the color from the image and just shows the luminosity values (lightness and darkness). Hence it makes it appear black and white. Hue is an offshoot of the Color blend mode, but interacts with the underlying layer a little differently. Finally, I copied-and-pasted a graphic from another image to finish things off.

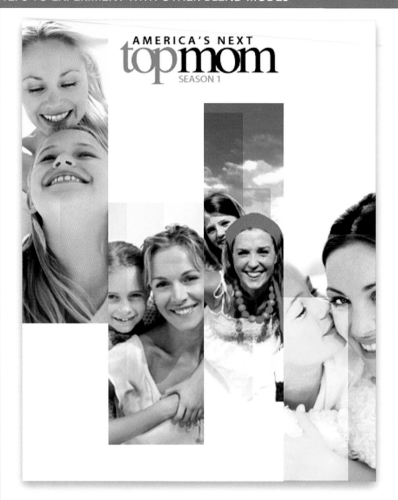

LAYER BLEND MODES FOR PHOTOGRAPHERS

HOW A FEW SIMPLE BLEND MODES CAN HELP ENHANCE YOUR PHOTOS

What I really like about blend modes is the fact that they don't change the actual pixels in your image. They just change the way things appear onscreen. As a photographer, this is a big deal because we want to be creative, yet we always want the flexibility to change things as a photo evolves. Blend modes are a great way to get the best of both of those worlds when it comes to enhancing your photos. In this tutorial, we're going to cover a few common examples of how blend modes can help photographers.

STEP 1: PROBLEM: DARK OR UNDEREXPOSED PHOTOS

©FOTOLIA/YURI ARCURS

One of the first ways you'll see blend modes can help with photos is when you have a photo with a dark or underexposed area. In our example here, we have a really common problem with portraits taken outdoors. The eye socket area of the person on the right shows up a little shadowy compared to the rest of his face. Because of the shape of our forehead and face, an overhead light source doesn't reach the eyes as much as other areas. Again, this is a really common problem that a blend mode can help.

STEP 2: DUPLICATE THE DARK AREA AND CHANGE THE BLEND MODE TO SCREEN

Grab the Lasso tool (L) and make a quick selection around the eye sockets (select one eye, then press-and-hold the Shift key while you select the other eye to add it to the original selection). Press Command-J (PC: Ctrl-J) to duplicate the selection onto its own layer, so now you'll have two layers in the Layers panel. Then, change the blend mode of the top layer to Screen. Because Screen is a lightening blend mode, it has the effect of lightening everything on that layer.

TIP: You can use the keyboard shortcut Option-Shift-S (PC: Alt-Shift-S) to switch to the Screen blend mode quickly.

STEP 3: REDUCE THE OPACITY OR ERASE AWAY ANY AREAS THAT ARE TOO LIGHT

Yeah, I know. He looks like a raccoon now. You could stop here if you wanted a good prank to play on your friends, but let's assume you want to move on. Select the Eraser tool (E), then click on the brush thumbnail in the Options Bar, and choose a small, soft-edged brush from the Brush Picker. Click-and-drag to erase away the areas that don't need the lightening effect. Finally, try reducing the opacity of the layer to about 50% to help it blend in better with the original layer below it.

Another problem that blend modes can help is when you have a bright, faded area in a photo. Here I've opened a photo where the sky looks good, but the buildings are too bright. The first step is to duplicate the Background layer by pressing Command-J.

Change the blend mode of the duplicate layer to Multiply. Since Multiply is a darkening blend mode, this darkens everything in the photo. It may look just fine like that, so feel free to leave it alone. However, in this photo I think it's made the sky look too saturated and dark. Select the Magic Wand tool (press Shift-W until you have it) and click on the sky to select it. You may have to Shift-click again elsewhere in the sky to add other areas if the entire sky wasn't selected the first time.

Press the Delete (PC: Backspace) key to remove (or erase) the sky, then press Command-D (PC: Ctrl-D) to Deselect. The darkening effect of the Multiply blend mode should now just affect the buildings, so they have a little more punch to them. Feel free to reduce the opacity if the effect is too dark.

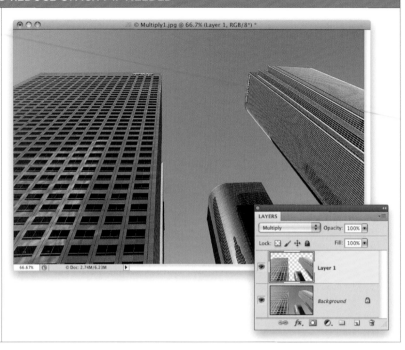

Here's another example of what Multiply can be used for: Open one of those cool, grungy black frame images, and you'll find most of them have white in the middle where the photo is supposed to go. To start, press Command-A (PC: Ctrl-A) to put a selection around the entire frame image.

STEP 8: COPY IT ONTO A PHOTO. CHANGE THE BLEND MODE TO MULTIPLY

Press Command-C (PC: Ctrl-C) to Copy the frame, then open another image and press Command-V (PC: Ctrl-V) to Paste it into that image. Go to Edit>Free Transform if you need to resize it to fit the photo. Then, change blend mode of the frame layer to Multiply, and Photoshop will automatically drop out the white and leave you with just the black frame around the photo. No selections, no nuthin'.

STEP 9: USE OVERLAY TO DARKEN A SKY AND BRIGHTEN A FOREGROUND

The last problem we're going to take a look at is when you have a photo with a bright sky and a dark foreground. This can usually be helped when taking the photo by using a graduated neutral density gradient filter on the camera. However, there are some things you can do after the fact in Photoshop to help, too. First, open the photo you want to enhance. Here's one where the sky is kinda bright, but the foreground is actually a little too dark.

STEP 10: CREATE A NEW LAYER. DRAW A BLACK-TO-WHITE GRADIENT ON IT

Create a new layer above the Background layer by clicking on the Create a New Layer icon at the bottom of the Layers panel. Then select the Gradient tool (G) from the Toolbox. Press Return (PC: Enter) to bring up the Gradient Picker. It'll show up wherever your cursor is on the screen. Then, choose the third gradient from the top left. It's one of the default gradients called Black, White. Finally, make sure you select the Linear Gradient option (the first icon to the right of the gradient thumbnail) in the Options Bar. Now, click-and-drag the gradient from the top of the photo to the bottom.

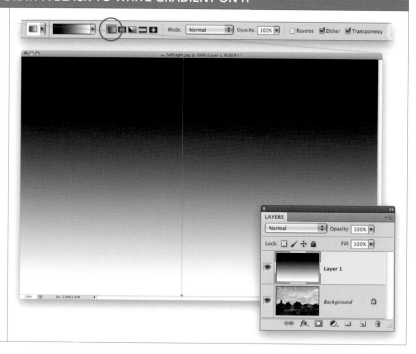

STEP 11: CHANGE THE BLEND MODE TO SOFT LIGHT. EXPERIMENT WITH OVERLAY, TOO

Remember those contrast-enhancing blend modes? They come in handy here because we want to blend based on the color of the gradient. Where the gradient is black, I want the photo below to be darkened, and where the gradient is white, I want it to be lightened. To make this happen, change the layer blend mode to Soft Light, and drop the opacity a little if you need to. You'll see the overall photo looks much better. I even erased the gradient on the rock up front with a low opacity Eraser tool, so it didn't look too bright.

TIP: Try Overlay too. It's a bit more saturated in this example, but sometimes looks better on photos that need color enhancement.

STEP 12: COPY A TEXTURE INTO A PHOTO. CHANGE THE BLEND MODE TO OVERLAY

Here's a totally different example to improve your photos with the Overlay or Soft Light blend mode: Open a photo and a texture image. It could be something you've downloaded or created in Photoshop, or you could just take a photo of a wall. Copy-and-paste the texture image into the photo. Change the texture layer to Overlay (or Soft Light), and it gives the photo a very rugged and faded style.

HOW DO I...

CHANGE A LAYER'S BLEND MODE?

Click on the layer to select it, then click on the blend mode pop-up menu in the top left of the Layers panel and choose your blend mode.

CYCLE THROUGH ALL OF THE BLEND MODES WITH THE KEYBOARD?

Click on the layer you want to change the blend mode for, then press Shift-+ (plus sign) to cycle down the menu and Shift-– (minus sign) to go back up.

OPEN THE LAYER STYLE DIALOG WITH LAYER BLENDING OPTIONS?

Double-click on the layer in the Layers panel.

QUICKLY CHANGE TO THE MULTIPLY BLEND MODE?

Press Option-Shift-M (PC: Alt-Shift-M).

QUICKLY CHANGE TO THE SCREEN BLEND MODE?

Press Option-Shift-S (PC: Alt-Shift-S).

QUICKLY CHANGE TO THE SOFT LIGHT BLEND MODE?

Press Option-Shift-F (PC: Alt-Shift-F).

CHANGE LAYER OPACITY WITH THE KEYBOARD?

Type the first number of the layer opacity setting you want. For 50%, type 5. For 35%, quickly type 35. (To use this keyboard shortcut, be sure you don't have a tool selected that has a percentage setting in the Options Bar.)

CHAPTER THREE

ADJUSTMENT LAYERS

At this point, you've seen how useful layers are for making adjustments to your images. But we've only been working with regular layers. There's also something in Photoshop called an adjustment layer. It's a different type of layer that has really changed the way people edit their images, because they let you work non-destructively. Even better, adjustment layers let you apply adjustments to selective parts of your photos so you don't have to apply the adjustments to the whole image—just part of it, if you want. They're way cool and they're easy to start using.

ADJUSTMENT LAYER BASICS

ADJUSTMENT LAYERS GIVE US THE ULTIMATE FLEXIBILITY WHEN IT COMES TO MAKING OUR PHOTOS LOOK BETTER

Why are adjustment layers so cool? Let's say we have a photo that we'd like to turn into a black-and-white photo. Sure, you can use the Black & White adjustment under the Image>Adjustments menu, but when you apply it to your image, you've made a permanent change. So if you save the file, you'd never be able to go back and see your color image again. Well, most of those adjustments under the Image>Adjustments menu are also available as adjustment layers. These little layers do the same exact adjustment, but on a separate layer. Not only can you easily get back to your original image by using adjustment layers, but you can also easily change the settings if you change your mind later on.

STEP 1: OPEN A PHOTO OF AN OBJECT WHOSE COLOR YOU'D LIKE TO CHANGE

There are a ton of examples to use for adjustment layers. Let's start out by changing the color of an object in a photo. So, go ahead and open a photo that has something you'd like to change the color of.

Note: If you want to follow along using this image, you can download it from the website mentioned in the introduction.

Just so you can see where these adjustment layers are coming from, click on the Image menu and look under Adjustments. See all of the options there? These are the various color and tonal corrections that are available in Photoshop. However, if you add them through this menu, they're permanent changes to your image. This means you'd never have a good way to go back and change or delete an adjustment made to any of your images.

Now, let's compare that Adjustments submenu with the Adjustments panel (which was added in CS4, by the way). If you don't see it on the right side of the screen, then go to Window>Adjustments to open it. As you hover over the small icons (I know they're really small—don't get me started), the name of the adjustment appears at the top of the panel. Notice how most of the adjustments are the same exact ones that are under the Image>Adjustments submenu? The one key difference is that the Adjustments panel creates an adjustment layer that can always be changed.

STEP 4: ADD A HUE/SATURATION ADJUSTMENT

Since you're already there, click on the Hue/Saturation icon (it's the second one from the left in the second row) to add a Hue/Saturation adjustment layer. You'll see the panel change to display the Hue/Saturation options. First, I only want to change the blue colors in the photo, not all the colors, so I changed the pop-up menu above the sliders to Blues. Now, any changes will only affect the blue hues. Then, to actually change the color, drag the Hue setting to –135. That changes the color of the blue object in the center to green.

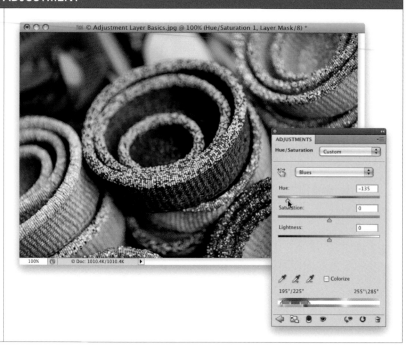

STEP 5: LOOK IN THE LAYERS PANEL TO SEE THE NEW LAYER

After you make the change, look over in the Layers panel. You'll see there's a new layer above the Background layer. That's the adjustment layer. The adjustment has essentially been applied to a separate layer, not the original photo. You can see this by looking closely at the Background layer thumbnail—the middle is still blue, not green, even though it looks green onscreen.

STEP 6: HIDE THE ADJUSTMENT LAYER TO SEE THE ORIGINAL

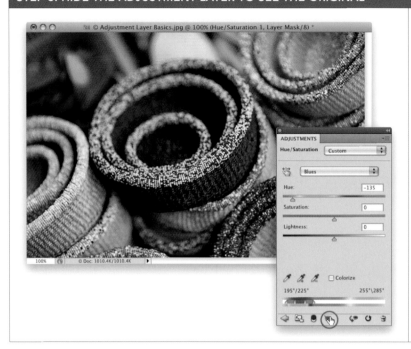

Adjustment layers work a lot like regular layers do. They have an opacity setting, you can rename them, and you can even hide them. Try it. You can, of course, do all of this in the Layers panel, but you can also do things right in the Adjustments panel. Try clicking on the little Eye icon at the bottom of the Adjustments panel and now you'll see your original photo that is underneath the adjustment layer in the Layers panel. The original blue color is all safe and sound.

STEP 7: SAVE THE LAYERED FILE AND REOPEN IT LATER. EDIT THE ADJUSTMENT LAYER

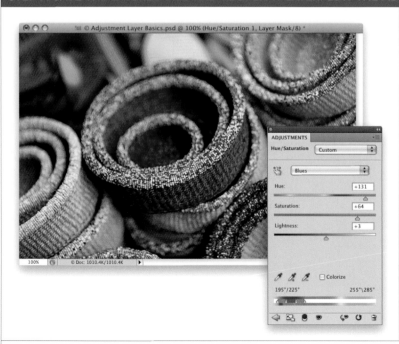

Let's assume you're done working. Save this image in the Photoshop PSD format under the File>Save As menu. Now, participate in a little role-playing game with me for a moment. Assume you show this to a client and they say they'd prefer the middle to be red instead. All you have to do is open the same PSD file and double-click on the adjustment layer's thumbnail in the Layers panel. The Adjustments panel will open and you'll see it remembers the settings you entered last time. To change them, just drag the sliders to something else. That's it. With adjustment layers you've always got a way out and a way to go back and change the settings.

MAKING SELECTIVE ADJUSTMENTS

IT DOESN'T HAVE TO BE ALL OR NOTHING WITH ADJUSTMENT LAYERS. YOU CAN SELECTIVELY CHANGE THINGS TOO!

Hey, what you just saw in the previous tutorial is pretty darn cool. Always having the ability to go and edit your adjustments at a later date is very powerful stuff. However, let's face it, the all or nothing factor of an adjustment can be limiting. Let's say that you have a photo where the sky looks great but the foreground is just too dark. You can always add a Levels adjustment layer to brighten the foreground but it's going to brighten the sky, too. Probably to the point where it's too bright, right? However, with adjustment layers you can selectively make adjustments to certain areas in your photos without affecting the whole thing.

STEP 1: OPEN A PHOTO WHERE ONLY ONE AREA NEEDS TO BE FIXED

Open a photo where one part of the photo looks fine but another area needs some work. In this case, I have a landscape photo, and I think the barn is too dark compared to the rest of the photo.

MATT KLOSKOWSKI

STEP 2: ADD A LEVELS ADJUSTMENT LAYER TO BRIGHTEN THE FOREGROUND

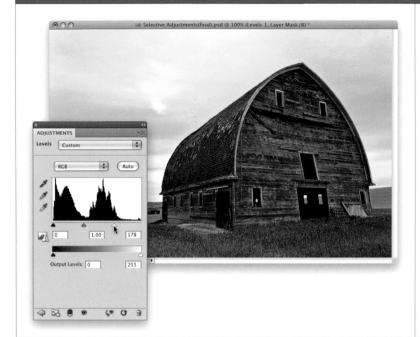

Go to the Adjustments panel and click on the Levels icon (the second one from the left in the top row). Now drag the white Input Levels slider under the histogram toward the left. Notice how everything in the photo gets brighter. In fact, we lose a lot of the detail in the clouds when we do this. We can fix this, though. Go ahead and click the Trash icon at the bottom right of the Adjustments panel to cancel that change, and let's start over.

STEP 3: FIRST, MAKE A SELECTION OF THE AREA YOU WANT TO BRIGHTEN

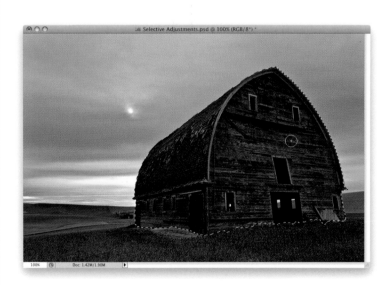

So, you've seen what happens when you just apply the Levels adjustment to the whole photo. This time, grab the Quick Selection tool (W) and click-and-drag over the barn to make a selection of the area you want to modify.

Note: Don't forget, as I mentioned in the introduction to the book, I recorded a video that goes over selections (since this book is about layers). You can find it at www.kelbytraining.com/books/layerscs5.

Go back and click the Levels icon in the Adjustments panel again. Drag the white Input Levels slider over toward the left just like you did before. I've dragged mine until the white point reads 148. Notice how only the area you selected in Step 3 gets brighter (the barn in this example)? The sky doesn't change.

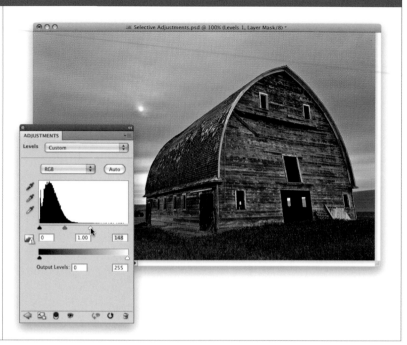

So, how did this happen? What's the deal? Well, take a look at that little white-and-black thumbnail next to the Levels adjustment layer thumbnail in the Layers panel. This is a layer mask (it's circled in red here). If you recall from the previous tutorial, when we changed the color with a Hue/Saturation adjustment, that layer mask was all white. Here's a screen capture of the Layers panel from the previous tutorial and the one from our example here to compare. See how the one from the earlier tutorial is all white, but the one from this tutorial shows white only in the area we made a selection on?

STEP 6: BLACK HIDES THE ADJUSTMENT AND SHOWS THE LAYER THAT IS DIRECTLY UNDERNEATH IT

The main thing to remember here is that the color (black or white) that you see on the little thumbnail actually matters. When it's all white, we see the effects of the adjustment layer over the entire photo. Wherever it's black, though, the effects of the adjustment layer get hidden and the original photo underneath the adjustment layer will show through. So, here the white is our selection of the barn and shows us our Levels adjustment, while the black is over the sky and grass areas and shows us the sky and grass from the Background layer.

STEP 7: TOGGLE THE ADJUSTMENT LAYER ON AND OFF TO SEE A BEFORE/AFTER

You can click the little Eye icon to the left of the Levels adjustment layer to hide the adjustment effects and look at the before image. Then click where the Eye icon was to show the adjustment again.

Before

After

fx ◻ ◕ ▢ ▢

SUPER FLEXIBLE ADJUSTMENTS

OKAY, NOW FOR THE REALLY COOL STUFF. ADJUSTMENT LAYERS HAVE ONE MORE SUPER COOL, FLEXIBLE FEATURE

So far you've seen that adjustment layers can stand on their own and apply an adjustment to the entire layer. And you've seen that you can make a selection to restrict the areas that an adjustment layer can affect. Adjustment layers have one more super cool, flexible feature to work with: brushes. While selections are great, brushes give you the ultimate flexibility. By using a brush on the adjustment layer, you can specifically apply the adjustment to the exact areas you want by painting them with black instead of filling a selection with black. It's the same concept but *way* more controlled and *way* easier.

STEP 1: OPEN A PHOTO THAT NEEDS AN ADJUSTMENT IN A SPECIFIC AREA

Open a photo that needs an adjustment in a specific area. In this case, the woman and her baby seem dark and don't really stand out from the background in the photo.

TIP: As you can see, I'm using a photo of people for this example. This could just as easily be a landscape photo similar to the ones we've looked at in this chapter, where some portion of the foreground is too dark and you want to lighten it. Just thought I'd mention that. You can read on now.

MATT KLOSKOWSKI

STEP 2: ADD A CURVES ADJUSTMENT LAYER TO BRIGHTEN THE PHOTO

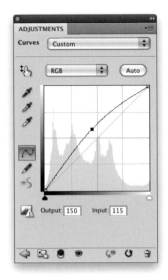 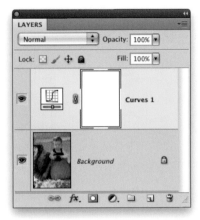

This time around, let's add a Curves adjustment layer to brighten the woman and her baby. Click on the Curves icon in the Adjustments panel (it's the third icon in the top row). Click in the middle of the diagonal line (the curve) and drag it upward and to the left. If you're not sure how far upward to drag right now, it's totally fine, because we can come back and adjust it later. You should see the new Curves adjustment layer appear in the Layers panel above the Background layer.

STEP 3: SELECT THE BRUSH TOOL AND CHOOSE A SEMI-LARGE, SOFT-EDGED BRUSH

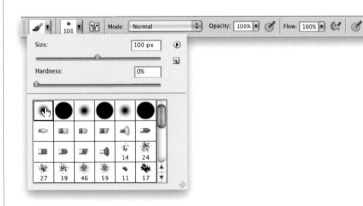

Now, the whole photo got brighter, but what we really want is for the woman and her baby to be brighter and the rest of the image the way it was. To make this happen, let's paint with black on the adjustment layer over the background to bring back the original dark photo in certain areas. First, select the Brush tool (B) from the Toolbox. Click on the brush thumbnail up in the Options Bar, and choose a large, soft-edged brush from the Brush Picker. Make sure your Foreground color is set to black (if black is your Background color instead, press X to switch them).

Note: Don't forget to check out the video I did on brushing basics that I mentioned in the book's introduction.

STEP 4: PAINT ON THE BACKGROUND TO DARKEN IT

Click once on the Curves adjustment layer's mask thumbnail to
make sure it's active (you'll see a
thin black frame around the corners). Start clicking-and-dragging
on the background in the photo
with the Brush tool. Normally, this
would paint black on the photo.
However, we're working on the
layer mask, so it's different. This
paints black on the layer mask next
to the Curves adjustment layer
thumbnail. By painting with black,
you'll be bringing back the original
background from the Background
layer under the Curves adjustment
layer (which was darker, by the
way). If you mess up, just press X
to switch your Foreground color to
white, and paint over the mistake.

STEP 5: CONTINUE PAINTING ON THE LAYER MASK UNTIL ALL THE BACKGROUND IS DARK AGAIN

Continue to paint until all of the
background area looks darker
again. You can always look at
the layer mask thumbnail on the
Curves adjustment layer to get a
glimpse of any white areas that
may still be left. You may also need
to zoom in and reduce your brush
size as you get close to the faces
and edges of the woman and
baby, so you can be more precise.
This works just like the previous
tutorial did, except we're painting
with black instead of filling a selection with black. Photoshop doesn't
care how you get black on the
layer mask, though. As long as it's
black, the original layer under the
adjustment layer will show through.

STEP 6: CLICK ON THE ADJUSTMENT LAYER'S THUMBNAIL TO TWEAK THE CURVE

Finally, remember how we weren't sure how much to drag the curve back in Step 2? You can always click on the Curves adjustment layer's thumbnail in the Layers panel and tweak the curve more. Since you've already done the work of hiding the Curves adjustment from the background so it only affects the people, any changes you make to the curve will be like turning a light brighter or darker on them. You can see exactly how much you want them to stand out from the background. I told you this stuff was cool!

Before

After

SOME MORE ADJUSTMENT LAYER IDEAS

ONCE YOU START USING ADJUSTMENT LAYERS, IT'S HARD TO STOP. HERE ARE A FEW MORE IDEAS

Trust me, once you start using adjustment layers, a whole new world of creative possibilities opens up. In fact, just about everything you do to fix or enhance your photos touches something up in that Image>Adjustments submenu. So, why not go ahead and use an adjustment layer for it instead? Here, I'll show you some quick examples of adjustment layers.

EXAMPLE 1: CREATING A BLACK-AND-WHITE IMAGE

The Black & White adjustment in the Adjustments panel (the fourth icon from the left in the second row) is probably the fastest (and easiest) way to create a black-and-white photo. Just click the Black & White icon and Photoshop removes all the color. Then, move any of the sliders to make the corresponding color lighter or darker. For example, if I move the Green slider to the left, it makes the trees darker (they were green). If I move it to the right, it makes them brighter.

MATT KLOSKOWSKI

EXAMPLE 2: BLACK AND WHITE WITH A TOUCH OF COLOR

If you want that sepia-tinted look, then turn on the Tint checkbox at the top of the Black & White options in the Adjustments panel. That adds a touch of color to the photo to give it a slightly tinted look. You can click on the color swatch next to the Tint checkbox to change the intensity of the color, as well as the tint color itself.

EXAMPLE 3: SEMI-BLACK-AND-WHITE EDGY LOOK

One more idea with the Black & White adjustment is to add the adjustment layer just like we did in the first example (with no tint). You'll see the Black & White adjustment layer in your Layers panel, and remember, it has all the qualities that regular layers have, so you can change things like opacity and blend mode. Try changing the blend mode of the adjustment layer to Overlay. It gives the photo a semi-desaturated look, and it's got a much edgier feel to it. It's great for sports and dramatic portraits. It's probably not good for puppies, kids, and warm-and-fuzzy-type photos.

EXAMPLE 4A: ENHANCING AND BOOSTING COLOR SATURATION

One of my favorite adjustments is Vibrance. If it sounds familiar, you may have seen it inside Camera Raw or in Photoshop Lightroom. It's an awesome adjustment for boosting color. What makes it really useful is that it only boosts colors in the photo that really need it. It tends to leave skin, and colors that are already properly saturated, alone.

©FOTOLIA/MONKEY BUSINESS

EXAMPLE 4B: COMPARE VIBRANCE WITH SATURATION

You'll notice that Vibrance did a great job of boosting the color in the kids' clothes, but it didn't saturate the skin tones. Compare that with the Saturation adjustment (which is what we had to use before Vibrance), which adds a bit of a sunburn effect to every person it touches, and makes the rest of the colors look a bit clownish.

EXAMPLE 5: SELECTIVELY ADDING COLOR

Here's another popular technique: you can create a black-and-white photo and then selectively add back color. It's great for really drawing someone in to look at the subject and makes for a very dramatic effect. First, convert your photo to black and white (like we did in the first example in this tutorial). Then paint with a black brush on the areas you want to bring back into color. In this example, the bouquet is the subject we want to paint on to show the color again. I just love this technique!

EXAMPLE 6: CHANGING THE MOOD OR FEEL OF A PHOTO

The Photo Filter adjustment layer is great for totally changing the mood or feel of a photo. It simulates the effect of traditional warming and cooling filters that used to be attached to the end of a lens. In this example, just open a photo that needs a little something extra. Then add a Photo Filter adjustment layer. Choose one of the warming filters to enhance the effect of that great early morning light.

EXAMPLE 7: TRY ONE OF THE COOLING FILTERS FOR THE OPPOSITE EFFECT

Another option with the Photo Filter adjustment on the previous page is to use a cooling filter. This has the opposite effect of the warming filter. It tends to make a photo appear very cool. Look how it totally changes the warm mood and feel in this photo and makes it appear like it was a cold day.

EXAMPLE 8: VINTAGE EFFECT

You can use adjustment layers to create a vintage effect, too. Try adding a Hue/Saturation adjustment layer first and reduce the Saturation to about –50 to take some of the color out of the photo. Then add a Color Balance adjustment layer on top. Leave the Tone set to Midtones, and move the bottom slider toward Yellow, to add that golden look. Then move the middle slider toward Green, which helps give that old vintage feel. Finally, move the top slider toward Red to bring back a little color in the skin tones, if your photo has people in it. Then, switch the Tone to Shadows, move the middle slider toward Green to +12 and the bottom slider toward Blue to +18.

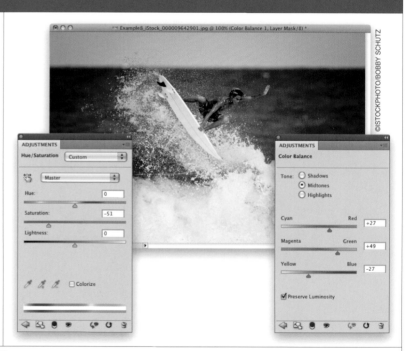

FIX ONE PHOTO—FIX 'EM ALL!

NOT ONLY ARE ADJUSTMENT LAYERS FLEXIBLE, BUT THEY CAN ALSO SAVE YOU A TON OF TIME

I flat-out love features that save me time. So far, I've been showing you how adjustment layers are great, wonderful, flexible, and all that stuff. Put all that aside for a minute, though, and take a look at a technique with adjustment layers that'll save you a ton of time if you're working on a bunch of photos that were shot in similar conditions.

STEP 1: OPEN ONE PHOTO FROM A GROUP OF PHOTOS THAT NEED ADJUSTING

MATT KLOSKOWSKI

Open a photo that has a color or lighting problem. This technique works best when you have several photos with the same problem. In this example, the combination of the white balance used and lighting in the room where the photo was taken gave the photo a yellow/green tint.

STEP 2: ADD A CURVES ADJUSTMENT LAYER

Go to the Adjustments panel and click on the Curves icon to add a Curves adjustment layer. First, let's give the photo a little more punch. Click on the bottom half of the curve, and drag it downward (as shown here), then click-and-drag upward in the top half. This gives it that classic S-curve shape and gives the photo better contrast overall.

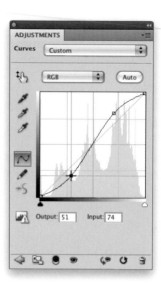

STEP 3: CLICK THE GRAY POINT EYEDROPPER ON SOMETHING THAT SHOULD BE GRAY

To fix the colorcast in the photo, select the gray point eyedropper (circled in red here). Then, click on something in the photo that should be gray. I know the countertop was gray (even though it doesn't appear that way here), so I'm going to click on that. The Curves adjustment balanced the color in the photo, so it looks much better now.

STEP 4: SAVE THE CURVES ADJUSTMENT AS A PRESET

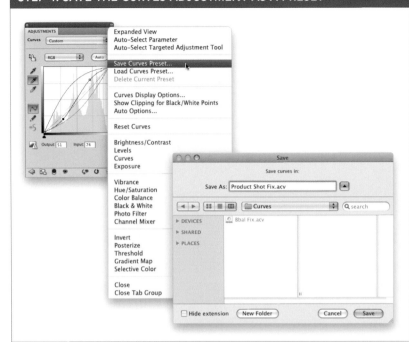

Since we'll want to use this same adjustment on some other photos later, let's save it as a preset. Click on the down-facing arrow in the top right of the Adjustments panel, and from the flyout menu, choose Save Curves Preset. Give it a descriptive name and click Save.

STEP 5: OPEN OTHER PHOTOS THAT WERE SHOT IN SIMILAR CONDITIONS

At this point, you've adjusted one photo. However, we have a couple more photos that were taken in the same exact lighting conditions, but we don't want to go in and re-create that Curves adjustment layer for each photo. That's why we created a preset in the last step. Now that same adjustment and its settings are just a click away. Open the other photos that were shot in the same conditions. As you can see, these suffer from the same colorcast and lack of contrast.

On one of the photos, go to the Adjustments panel. Don't click on the Curves icon, though. Instead, click on the right-facing arrow next to Curves Presets below the icons to expand that section. Then simply scroll to the preset you just created and click on it, and Photoshop will apply that same exact Curves adjustment to this photo. With just one click, you've fixed that photo too. Now, just do the same thing for the last photo.

fx ▢ ◐ ▢ ▢

THE ADJUSTMENT LAYER BLEND MODE TRICK

YOU DON'T HAVE TO DO ANYTHING TO AN ADJUSTMENT LAYER TO MAKE IT USEFUL

Okay, I'm going to get a little techie on you here. But trust me, I'm doing it for your own good. I'm getting techie because it'll help you be more creative in the long run—you'll see why. Many times, when you're working on a layered document, you'll duplicate a layer and change its blend mode to something like Multiply or Screen just like we did in Chapter 2. Then you'll selectively erase part of that duplicate layer (or better yet, use layer masks, which we'll talk more about in the next chapter). Here's the thing: the second you duplicate that layer, your image is taking up twice as much space on your computer as it did before. Here, I'm going to show you how you can avoid this.

STEP 1: IF YOU BELIEVE ME, THEN SKIP TO STEP 2. IF NOT, THEN TRY A QUICK TEST

If you read the intro and you believe how much space just one duplicate copy of a layer takes up, then go ahead and skip to Step 2. If you don't believe me, then try a quick test: Open a photo right from your camera. In my case, I shoot with a 10-megapixel camera in RAW mode, so here's one of the photos opened in Photoshop. I saved it as a PSD file to my desktop when it had just one layer. Then I duplicated the Background layer by pressing Command-J (PC: Ctrl-J) and saved another copy to my desktop when it had two layers. When compared, the image with two layers was a whopping 55.7 MB larger than the image with one layer. Enough said?

STEP 2: OPEN A PHOTO THAT WOULD BENEFIT FROM ONE OF THE BLEND MODE TUTORIALS IN CHAPTER 2

Go ahead and open a photo that would benefit from one of the blend modes (Screen or Multiply) discussed in Chapter 2. In this example, I'm using the same exact photo of the tall buildings and the blue sky. Remember, we used the Multiply blend mode to darken the buildings a little.

MATT KLOSKOWSKI

STEP 3: ADD A LEVELS OR CURVES ADJUSTMENT LAYER, BUT THIS TIME DON'T CHANGE THE SETTINGS

Go to the Adjustments panel and click on the Levels or Curves icon to add an adjustment layer on top of the Background layer. It actually doesn't matter which adjustment layer you use, since we're not actually going to change the settings. Just add any adjustment layer and don't change a thing in its options.

STEP 4: CHANGE THE BLEND MODE OF THE ADJUSTMENT LAYER TO MULTIPLY

Change the blend mode of the adjustment layer to Multiply. This will darken the entire image onscreen. What's important to note here is that this change has the same exact effect as duplicating the Background layer and changing its blend mode to Multiply, like we did back in Chapter 2.

STEP 5: USE A SELECTION TOOL TO REVEAL PART OF THE ORIGINAL LAYER BELOW

Use the selection tool you are most comfortable with to make a selection of the sky, make sure your Foreground color is set to black, and press Option-Delete (PC: Alt-Backspace) to fill the selection with black. When saved as a PSD file, the file size is considerably smaller than it was with two layers. Smaller file size means less hard drive space used, less RAM used, and overall less processing power needed for your image.

HOW DO I...

DUPLICATE AN ADJUSTMENT LAYER?

Just like you would any other layer: press Command-J (PC: Ctrl-J).

RESET THE SETTINGS INSIDE THE ADJUSTMENTS PANEL?

To reset your settings when you're in the Adjustments panel, click on the Reset icon (the second from the right) at the bottom of the panel.

PREVIEW THE BEFORE/AFTER EFFECTS OF THE ADJUSTMENT LAYER WHILE IN THE PANEL?

Click on the Eye icon at the bottom of the Adjustments panel, or to the left of the adjustment layer in the Layers panel, to toggle the adjustment on/off.

SET MY FOREGROUND/BACKGROUND COLORS TO THEIR DEFAULTS (BLACK AND WHITE) FOR PAINTING WITH THE BRUSH TOOL?

Press the letter D to set your Foreground and Background colors to their defaults (black for the Foreground color and white for the Background color). These may be reversed on an adjustment layer.

QUICKLY FILL A LAYER MASK OR SELECTION ON A LAYER MASK WITH THE FOREGROUND COLOR?

Set your Foreground color to the desired color by pressing D for the defaults or clicking on the Foreground color swatch at the bottom of the Toolbox and choosing a color from the Color Picker. Then, press Option-Delete (PC: Alt-Backspace) to fill the layer mask or selection.

QUICKLY FILL A LAYER MASK OR SELECTION ON A LAYER MASK WITH THE BACKGROUND COLOR?

Set your Background color to the desired color by pressing D for the defaults or clicking on the Background color swatch at the bottom of the Toolbox and choosing a color from the Color Picker. Then, press Command-Delete (PC: Ctrl-Backspace) to fill the layer mask or selection.

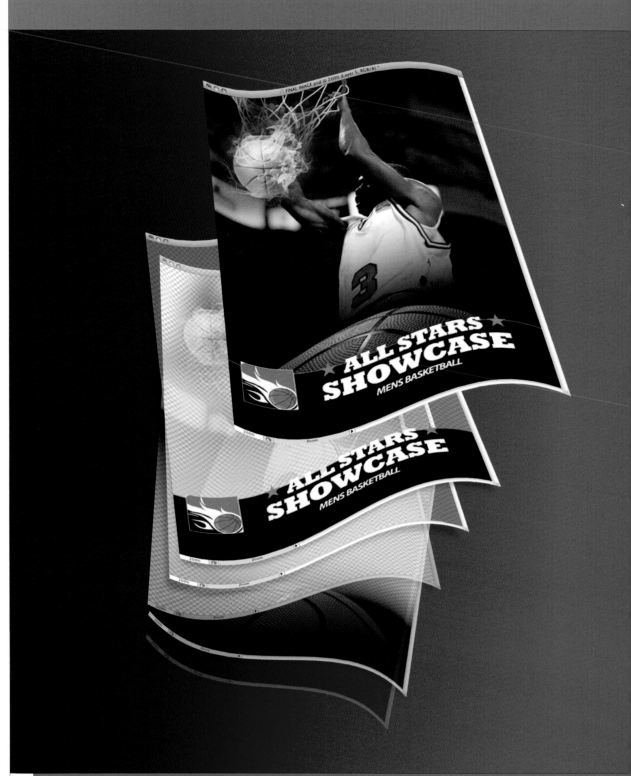

CHAPTER FOUR

LAYER MASKS

I'm going to start this chapter intro out with a bold statement. In fact, if there's one chapter intro you want to make sure you read, it's this one. Okay, so are you ready for my bold statement? Because if you're not, I'll wait a moment—no, really, it's okay. Okay, I guess I'd better make my bold statement before I just flat out annoy you. Here it is: you already know what a layer mask is. Yep, as long as you read through and understood what we did with adjustment layers in Chapter 3, you already know all about layer masks. If you didn't read Chapter 3, then I take my bold statement back. You have no idea what a layer mask is. But you will, if you go back and read Chapter 3 and then follow it up with this chapter. Why? Because layer masks are one of the most important things you can learn when it comes to layers. It's a topic that I've seen a lot of people try to avoid. But, once you figure them out, you'll wonder how you ever got along without them.

fx

LAYER MASK BASICS

LAYER MASKS LET YOU NON-DESTRUCTIVELY ERASE AWAY AREAS FROM ONE LAYER TO REVEAL THE LAYERS BELOW

Let me start out by saying that if you didn't read the chapter intro on the previous page, then stop right now and go read it. I made a very profound statement there and I think it's important that you read it before continuing. If you don't, then the rest of this chapter just won't be the same for you. So go read it...now. I'll wait. Okay, you're back and I bet you feel much better about embarking on your journey to learn all about layer masks. Now, in that chapter intro, I said that you already know what a layer mask is. You do! That little white thumbnail that kept getting added next to each adjustment layer we added in Chapter 3 is a layer mask. The difference between them and what we're about to do here is that adjustment layers automatically include a layer mask with them. A regular layer doesn't. But, it takes just one click to get the same effect.

STEP 1: OPEN TWO PHOTOS THAT YOU'D LIKE TO COMBINE

In order to really take advantage of layer masks, you need to have at least two layers. So go ahead and open two images that you'd like to combine. You can download the images shown here from the website I mentioned in the book's introduction.

©FOTOLIA/GIORDANO AITA

©FOTOLIA/GIORDANO AITA

STEP 2: COMBINE THE IMAGES SO THEY'RE IN THE SAME DOCUMENT

Press-and-hold the Shift key, and use the Move tool (V) to drag one photo from its document onto the other one (using the Shift key keeps the images lined up). In this example, I'm going to drag the photo of the soccer player onto the image of the soccer field. Now that photo's document has two layers. Once you've got the photo moved, you can close the original so you're left with only the document with two layers.

STEP 3: MAKE A SELECTION OF THE AREA WE WANT TO KEEP

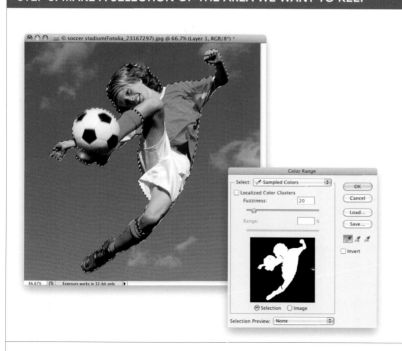

One of the main things to understand about layer masks is that they work closely with selections. So, in our example, let's make a selection of the boy. Click on the top layer, then go to Select>Color Range. Set the Fuzziness slider to 20. Then, move your cursor over the orange shirt and click on it with the eyedropper. In Color Range, Photoshop makes selections based on color (I know, duh!). You'll notice it doesn't select the whole shirt, though. Try pressing-and-holding the Shift key to go into Add mode and Shift-click in a bunch of places all over the boy to select all of him. Just stay away from clicking on anything blue (the sky, the top of his socks). Click OK when you're done.

STEP 4: ADD A LAYER MASK TO HIDE THE BACKGROUND ON THE TOP LAYER

When you have a selection active, adding a layer mask tells Photoshop that you want to keep the selected area visible and hide everything that isn't selected. In our case, the soccer player is selected, so he'll stay visible, but the rest of the photo will get hidden, right? Try it. Make sure the top layer is still active and click on the Add Layer Mask icon at the bottom of the Layers panel (circled here). You'll see the blue sky disappear, but the soccer player (which is what we selected earlier) is still there.

STEP 5: NOTICE HOW A REGULAR LAYER MASK LOOKS JUST LIKE THE ADJUSTMENT LAYER ONE

When you clicked on the Add Layer Mask icon, you saw that Photoshop added a little white thumbnail next to the layer thumbnail in your Layers panel. This is a layer mask. See how it looks just like the one that we saw in Chapter 3 whenever we added an adjustment layer? The only real difference here is that you've got to manually add a layer mask to a regular layer. When you use adjustment layers, Photoshop automatically adds the layer mask. But they're essentially the same exact thing and function the same way.

Adjustment layer with mask

Regular layer with mask

STEP 6: WHITE ON THE LAYER MASK SHOWS THE TOP LAYER; BLACK REVEALS WHAT'S UNDERNEATH

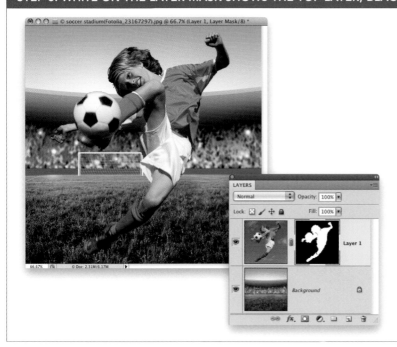

It's all about black and white. That's all layer masks care about. To see how things are working here, take a look at the layer mask thumbnail. Wherever it's white, we can see the soccer player layer (the layer that holds the actual layer mask). Where you see black on the layer mask, you see through the soccer player layer to whatever is underneath it in the Layers panel (in this case, the soccer stadium). That's the single most important thing to understand about layer masks: black and white. White shows you whatever is on the layer that the layer mask is on. Black hides that layer and shows you whatever is below it in the layer stacking order.

STEP 7: THEY LOOK LIKE SEPARATE OBJECTS, BUT THEY'RE REALLY ON TOP OF EACH OTHER

Another way to visualize what a layer mask is doing is to imagine that the mask is on top of the layer you put it on. Even though they appear side-by-side in the Layers panel, you could put the layer mask on top of the image thumbnail and it would fit perfectly. It would almost look like a stencil or an outline that you would cut away with scissors. The white would be the shape you want to keep from the photo, and the black would be what you'd cut away to reveal whatever was below the soccer player.

STEP 8: NOTHING IS PERMANENT WITH LAYER MASKS

The biggest advantage of layer masks is that nothing is permanent. Even though it looks like we've deleted the sky around the soccer player, it's still there. Go ahead, look at the layer thumbnail and you'll see it looks exactly the same. Nothing was deleted—it's just hidden. Layer masks are non-destructive and always give you a way out. Just to demonstrate really quickly, click once on the layer mask thumbnail (not the layer thumbnail) to select it. Then go to Edit>Fill. Set the Use pop-up menu to White and click OK to fill the mask with white again. Things are back to normal, as if nothing ever happened.

STEP 9: USE THE BRUSH TOOL TO FINE TUNE THE LAYER MASK

Go to Edit>Undo Fill to undo that last step, so the black-and-white layer mask is back. If you look closely, our selection from Step 3 wasn't perfect. A few areas are missing, but we'll take care of that. Remember, layer masks just care about one thing—black and white. It doesn't matter how black and white get there. Earlier, we created a selection before adding the mask, but you can also use a brush to get the ultimate flexibility and control. Click on the mask thumbnail, get the Brush tool (B), and choose a small, soft-edged brush. Set your Foreground color to white (remember, white keeps whatever is on this layer visible) and paint over the areas we missed. You'll see them reappear.

You can see I went a little over-board with the white brush. While I did bring back the parts of the soccer player that were missing, I also brought back parts of the sky. No sweat. Remember that black-and-white thing? Just switch your Foreground color to black, then paint on the mask again to hide those areas and reveal the stadium layer below.

TIP: When using layer masks, get used to the X key. Pressing X swaps your Foreground and Background colors, so you've got a quick way to switch from black to white or vice versa.

BEFORE AND AFTER

Before

After

fx ▢ ◐ ▢ ▨

THE ONLY LAYER MASK "GOTCHA"

THERE'S ONE LITTLE DIFFERENCE YOU NEED TO KNOW ABOUT REGULAR LAYER MASKS BEFORE MOVING ON

Okay, you got me. I lied earlier. Really, it was just a tiny lie. I said earlier that there was no difference between the layer mask that was added automatically with an adjustment layer and the layer mask that you add to a regular layer. Well, that's not totally true. There is a very small difference. When we added the adjustment layers, all you had to do was click anywhere on the adjustment layer to edit its layer mask. Well, with a regular layer mask, it actually matters where you click on the layer.

STEP 1: OPEN TWO PHOTOS TO BLEND TOGETHER

First, go ahead and open two photos. They could be of anything, but I take any chance I can to show off my two sons, Ryan and Justin. Select all of one of the photos (press Command-A [PC: Ctrl-A]), then copy-and-paste it into the other one by pressing Command-C (PC: Ctrl-C), switching to the other photo, and pressing Command-V (PC: Ctrl-V), so there are now two layers in one document. With the top layer active, click on the Add Layer Mask icon at the bottom of the Layers panel to add a layer mask to the top layer.

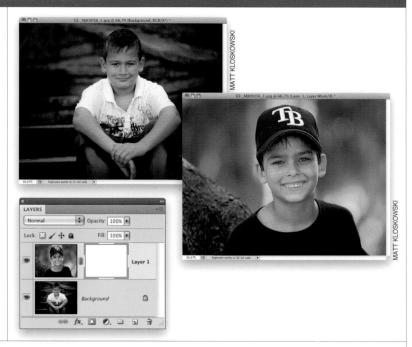

STEP 2: NOTICE THE TWO THUMBNAILS THAT APPEAR IN THE LAYERS PANEL ON THE LAYER WITH A MASK

Take a closer look at the top layer (the one with the mask). Notice how there are two thumbnails on that layer? One is the actual layer thumbnail that gives you a little preview of what is on that layer. The other is the layer mask itself.

STEP 3: CLICK ON THE LAYER THUMBNAIL TO SELECT IT

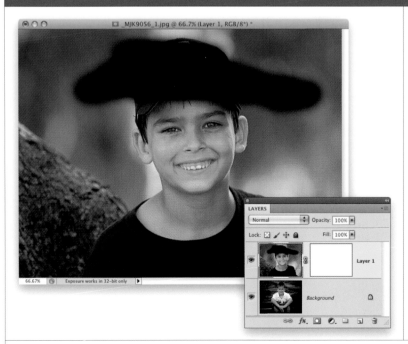

Click once on the actual layer thumbnail to select it. And I mean click on the thumbnail itself, not the highlighted area around it. If you look closely, you'll see a small black outline around the corners of the thumbnail. That's Photoshop's way of telling you that the layer is selected and ready to edit. If you were to get the Brush tool (B) and paint with black at this point, you'd be painting with black on the photo itself and you would see black brush strokes everywhere you paint.

STEP 4: CLICK ONCE ON THE LAYER MASK THUMBNAIL TO SELECT IT

This time, click once on the layer mask thumbnail to select it. Look closely again and you'll see that black outline now appears around the corners of the layer mask, not the layer thumbnail. Now paint with a black brush on the layer mask. Wherever you paint with black, you'll start hiding the photo on that layer and revealing the layer underneath it, as you see here.

STEP 5: IT MAKES A DIFFERENCE WHAT THUMBNAIL YOU SELECT AND PAINT ON

See how it makes a difference when it comes to what thumbnail you select in the Layers panel? That's why it's important to know that if you want to do something to the layer mask, you've got to actually click on that layer mask thumbnail. If you want to do something to the actual image or what you see on that layer, then click on the layer thumbnail. So, when you work with layer masks, if things aren't showing up like you thought they should, take a look over at the Layers panel and see which thumbnail is selected. Ninety percent of the time, that's the cause. Okay, now we can move on. See? I told you it was only a small lie.

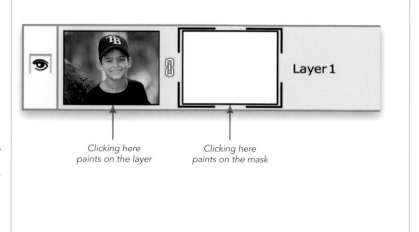

Clicking here paints on the layer

Clicking here paints on the mask

A DEEPER LOOK INTO LAYER MASKS

LET'S TAKE A DEEPER LOOK INTO LAYER MASKS AND SOME OF THE EXTRA THINGS YOU CAN DO WITH THEM

We're going to revisit the soccer player from a previous tutorial and do some other cool stuff with him. Layer masks have a lot of tiny features that make them easier to work with. Plus, back in Photoshop CS4, Adobe added an entire panel (the Masks panel) to help make working with layer masks easier and more intuitive.

STEP 1: OPEN THE PHOTOS FOR THE MASKING PROJECT. DRAG THE BOY INTO THE RIPPED IMAGE

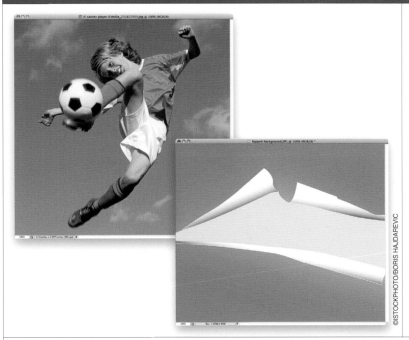

Go ahead and open the photos you'd like to combine. We'll revisit the soccer player from the first tutorial to create an image that looks like he's coming out of a ripped page. Just like in that tutorial, press-and-hold the Shift key, and use the Move tool (V) to drag the photo of the boy into the ripped image, so now you'll have two layers there.

STEP 2: USE THE QUICK SELECTION TOOL TO MAKE A SELECTION INSIDE THE RIPPED AREA

Click on the Eye icon next to the top layer to hide it, and click on the ripped image layer. The Quick Selection tool (W) combined with the new Refine Edge feature in Photoshop CS5 is one of the most powerful selection tools in Photoshop. Since it's a brush, you can just paint on the ripped area to select it. Be sure to use the Right and Left Bracket keys to resize the brush and get any areas you may have missed. If you select too much, just press-and-hold the Option (PC: Alt) key to go into Subtract mode and erase away the areas you don't need.

TIP: Don't forget about the selection primer tutorial online at www .kelbytraining.com/books/layerscs5.

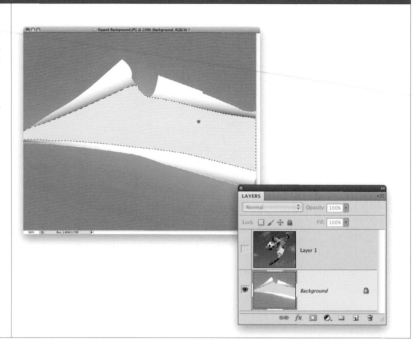

STEP 3: ADD A LAYER MASK TO THE LAYER WITH THE BOY ON IT TO HIDE THE REST OF THE PHOTO

Unhide the layer with the soccer player on it by clicking where the Eye icon used to be, then click on the layer to make it active. Click on the Add Layer Mask icon at the bottom of the Layers panel to add a mask to this layer. Since we have a selection active, Photoshop will hide whatever is not selected. Remember, when you have a selection, adding a layer mask will keep the selected area visible and hide whatever is not selected.

STEP 4: HIDE THE LAYER MASK. USE THE QUICK SELECTION TOOL TO SELECT THE REST OF THE BOY

At this point, we only have part of the soccer player visible in the ripped area. We need to get the rest of the soccer player showing through, too. Let's make another selection with the Quick Selection tool. This time, we'll select the soccer player, but only part of that layer is visible, right? It's because the rest of it is hidden by the mask. Well, Photoshop will let you temporarily turn the mask off, so you can see everything. Shift-click on the layer mask thumbnail, you'll see a big red X appear on it, and you'll be able to see the entire layer again. Now, use the Quick Selection tool to put a selection around the soccer player.

STEP 5: FILL THE SELECTION WITH WHITE

We need to add this selection to the existing layer mask, so the entire soccer player is visible through the ripped area. First, Shift-click on the layer mask thumbnail to unhide it. Then go to Edit>Fill. Select White in the Use pop-up menu and click OK to fill the selection with white. You've just added the soccer player to the layer mask, so now the sky and the soccer player are visible through the ripped section of the background photo. Press Command-D (PC: Ctrl-D) to get rid of your selection.

STEP 6: CHECK OUT THE MASKS PANEL. IT HELPS YOU CHANGE YOUR LAYER MASKS

Check out the Masks panel. It usually appears nested with the Adjustments panel, but you can go to Window>Masks to open it. This panel (added in Photoshop CS4) gives you an easy way to adjust your masks without having to know a lot of the secret handshakes that layer mask users used to memorize. The Density slider is like an Opacity slider for the mask. At 100% density, the mask is at full opacity. When you drag the Density slider below 100% though, you'll start to see whatever the layer mask is hiding. You'll even see the layer mask itself turn gray and approach white the closer you get to 0%. The Feather setting softens (or blurs) the edges of the mask (as seen here), so they don't appear too harsh.

STEP 7: USE THE MASKS PANEL TO REFINE THE SELECTION EDGE

Density and Feather are cool, but the real power of the Masks panel comes when you click the Mask Edge button, so go ahead and click it. If you look at our selection around the soccer player, you'll see it's not perfect. Without turning this into a selection book, the most powerful feature here is the Refine Radius tool (the little brush icon on the left side). Click on it to turn it on, then brush along any edges that seem too harsh or poorly selected (like the hair). Photoshop does some crazy computing, and most of the time it comes out looking amazing. Brush around any other areas and click OK when you're done. That's it. Photoshop was adjusting the mask as you made changes, so it should look a lot better now.

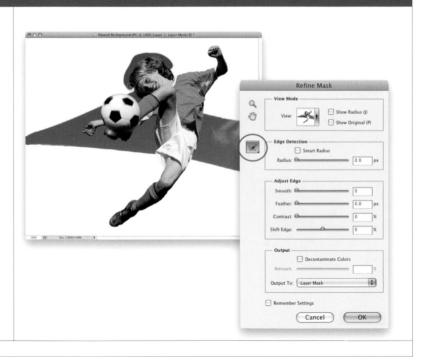

STEP 8: ADD A TEXTURE LAYER TO THE ORANGE BACKGROUND

Okay, the soccer player is looking good. But, I think the orange background is a little plain, so let's bring in a texture. Go ahead and open the other image for this tutorial if you want to follow along. It's a simple layer with hexagon shapes on it. Press-and-hold the Shift key (to keep it centered), grab the Move tool (V), click on the Hexagon layer, and drag it on top of our soccer player image. If it doesn't appear directly above the soccer player layer in the Layers panel, click on the layer and drag it to the top of the layer stack.

STEP 9: COPY THE MASK FROM ANOTHER LAYER SO WE CAN REUSE IT

You can probably tell that the hexagon texture we just dragged in covers the entire photo. We could go through the whole process of making selections and masks again to hide it, but instead, we'll do something that's a lot easier than that. We can copy masks from other layers. If you simply click-and-drag a mask, you can move it from one layer to another. But if you press-and-hold the Option (PC: Alt) key before you click-and-drag the mask, it makes a copy of it. Try it. Option-click-and-drag the mask from the soccer player layer to the hexagon layer. You've just made an exact dupli-cate of the mask on another layer.

STEP 10: USE THE MASKS PANEL TO INVERT THE MASK ON THE TEXTURE LAYER

We have one small problem: the mask that was on the soccer player was there to show us the soccer player through the ripped portion of the photo, and to hide everything else. That's why we now only see the hexagon texture over the soccer player and not the orange background. We want the opposite here. We want the hexagon to appear on the orange background. No problem. Make sure the layer mask thumbnail is selected. Then go to the Masks panel and click the Invert button. This turns everything that was black to white, and whatever was white turns black. It essentially reverses the mask and gives us just what we want.

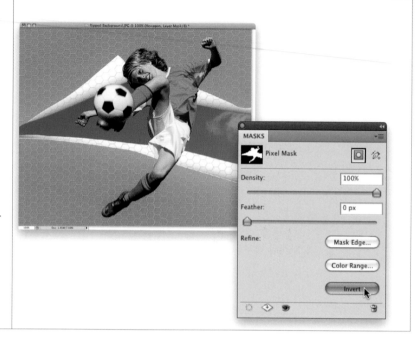

STEP 11: ADD A SHADOW BY MAKING A SELECTION FROM A LAYER

We're just about done. I think the soccer player looks a little flat, though, so let's add a drop shadow under him. First, remember that a layer mask is basically a selection. Many times they are created from a selection to start with, right? Well you can load that selection and make it visible again. So, let's load the soccer player's selection by first clicking on that layer, then Command-clicking (PC: Ctrl-clicking) on the layer mask thumbnail.

STEP 12: ADD A NEW LAYER. FILL THE SELECTION WITH BLACK. ADD A GAUSSIAN BLUR TO SOFTEN IT

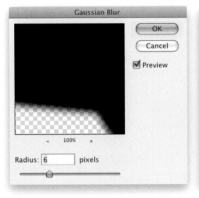

Now, we'll create a shadow for some depth. Click on the Background layer, then click on the Create a New Layer icon at the bottom of the Layers panel. Fill the selection with black by going to Edit>Fill, and selecting Black from the Use pop-up menu, then clicking OK. Press Command-D (PC: Ctrl-D) to Deselect. Now let's blur the selection a little to soften the edges. Go to Filter>Blur>Gaussian Blur and enter 6 or 7 pixels for the Radius setting. Click OK, and you should have a nice soft shadow emanating from behind the soccer player.

STEP 13: BREATHE FOR A MOMENT AND TAKE A LOOK AT WHAT'S GOING ON

Okay, breathe for a second. There are lots of layers and masking going on here. Notice that the black shadow only appears over the orange background. It doesn't show up on the sky at all. Why? Think about it for a second. The black shadow is on a layer below the soccer player, so we'll only see the glow, not the full black figure we created. Then, the mask on the layer above (the soccer player) only lets the sky and soccer player show through. So, anything we add on a layer below (like a shadow) won't show up on the sky (which is a good thing, because we don't want it there). It only shows on the ripped background image.

STEP 14: ERASE THE AREAS OF THE SHADOW WE DON'T NEED

You may have noticed the shadow emanates from behind the soccer player like he's glowing. Since it's a shadow, we only want it to cast in one direction (down and to the right). So add a layer mask to the shadow layer. It's all white, so nothing happens yet. Select the Brush tool (B), set your Foreground color to black, and paint away the left edges of the shadow. Try reducing the shadow layer's opacity to around 60% to soften the shadow even more.

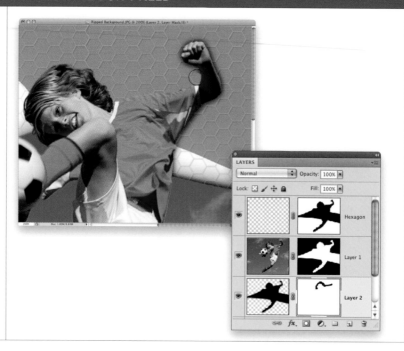

STEP 15: ADD ANY TEXT AND FINISHING TOUCHES

I finished things up here by adding some text. We'll cover using Type layers more in Chapter 5, but I've also provided an image with the layers, in case you want to add them, as well.

USING LAYER MASKS AUTOMATICALLY

YOU CAN AUTOMATICALLY CREATE LAYER MASKS BY MAKING A SIMPLE SELECTION

The title to this tutorial definitely doesn't do it justice, but I couldn't think of a better name. It's a way to automatically create layer masks simply by copying-and-pasting photos. The amount of flexibility you get helps out a lot when combining photos, so make sure you at least flip the page to see how cool an effect this is.

STEP 1: FIND A PHOTO WITH AN AREA IN IT THAT YOU'D LIKE TO REPLACE

Open two photos that you'd like to combine in some way. In this example, I'd like to place the photo of the snowy mountains inside the man's ski goggles. There's a little secret to layer masks that makes this really simple.

STEP 2: SWITCH TO THE PHOTO YOU WANT TO REPLACE IT WITH, SELECT ALL, AND COPY THE PHOTO

Start off with the photo that you want to use as the replacement area. In this example, we're using the photo of the mountain. Choose Select>All to select everything (or press Command-A [PC: Ctrl-A]), and then choose Edit>Copy (Command-C [PC: Ctrl-C]).

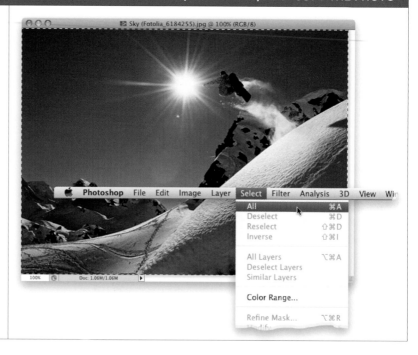

STEP 3: MAKE A SELECTION OF THE AREA YOU WANT TO REPLACE

Now, switch over to the photo of the man with the ski goggles. We need to first make a selection of the area we want to replace. Here, I used the Quick Selection tool (W) to click-and-drag across the lens inside the goggles to select it. If the selection spills over onto the face or the surrounding areas, press-and-hold the Option (PC: Alt) key and click on those areas to subtract them from the selection. Press Z to get the Zoom tool if you need a larger view.

Note: Don't forget I created a selections video tutorial for you over at www.kelbytraining.com/books/layerscs5. So, if you need a selections primer, go watch the video first.

STEP 4: USE PASTE INTO TO PASTE THE MOUNTAIN INTO THE SKI GOGGLES

Now click on the Edit menu and choose Paste Special>Paste Into (remember, we copied the mountain photo in Step 2). You've probably never used this one before, but it's really cool. See, it pastes the photo you have copied (in this case, the mountain) into the active selection. It makes sure that the photo only appears in the selection by creating a layer mask automatically. See how the name of this tutorial fits in? You've created a layer mask automatically just by using Edit>Paste Special>Paste Into.

STEP 5: USE THE MOVE TOOL TO REPOSITION THE PHOTO TO BETTER FIT INTO THE GOGGLES

Here's where it gets really cool, though: Select the Move tool from the Toolbox (or press V). Then click-and-drag the photo of the mountain around. Photoshop lets you move the photo to reposition it, but still keeps it inside the original selection. That's because the Paste Into command created that layer mask.

STEP 6: RESIZE AND WARP THE PHOTO TO MAKE IT APPEAR MORE REALISTIC

Even better, you can resize the photo without changing anything, too. Click the Edit menu and choose Free Transform (or press Command-T [PC: Ctrl-T]). Press-and-hold the Shift key and drag one of the corner handles in to make the photo fit better. Click-and-drag inside the box to move it. Then, from the Edit menu, choose Transform>Warp. Choose Inflate from the Warp pop-up menu on the left of the Options Bar, and bend the photo to match the distorted (bulged) perspective you'd probably see in the reflection of someone's goggles. Press Return (PC: Enter) when you're done to commit the transformation.

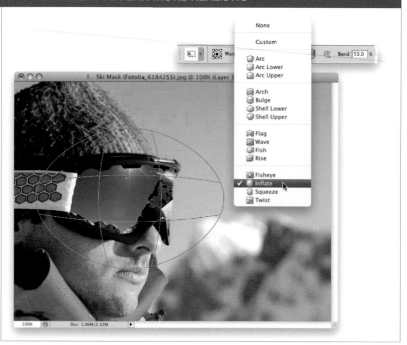

STEP 7: ADD A GRADIENT AND REDUCE THE OPACITY OF THE REFLECTION TO MAKE IT BLEND IN

Here's one last finishing touch that adds some depth to the flat reflec-tion: Get the Gradient tool (G), and up in the Options Bar, choose the default Black, White gradient from the Gradient Picker, click the Linear Gradient icon, and set the Mode to Soft Light. Then, click on the Lock Transparent Pixels icon near the top left of the Layers panel. Now, click-and-drag from the left side of the goggles to the far right, so the gradient darkens on the left and brightens on the right. If you look at the layer thumbnail, we did indeed add the gradient to the entire image, but because of the layer mask, you see it only over the goggles. I also reduced the layer's opacity to about 90% to fade the reflection a bit.

COMBINING MULTIPLE IMAGES

LAYER MASKS LET YOU COMBINE MULTIPLE IMAGES WITHOUT ERASING PARTS OF THE IMAGE

If you think back to Chapter 1, we combined several images together in "Using Multiple Layers" by bringing them all into the same document and erasing parts of each layer away. That example was great for showing how layers work with each other and how you can see through part of one layer to the layer under it. However, when it comes to real life, it's not that easy. You change your mind, the client changes his mind, or something just changes about the project, and you realize that permanently erasing away parts of a layer isn't a good thing. Mainly because you can't bring those erased pixels back. You'd have to start all over again if you want to change something. Well, now we're going to take a look at doing the same thing with layer masks. In fact, we're going to use the same example to see how it should be done. Trust me, this stuff rocks! Once you see how easy it is, I promise you that you'll never go back to that Eraser tool again.

STEP 1: OPEN THE PHOTOS THAT YOU'D LIKE TO BLEND TOGETHER

For starters, open the photos that you'd like to blend together.

STEP 2: CREATE A NEW DOCUMENT

Go to File>New to create a new document. Enter 5 inches for the Width, 7 inches for the Height, and 72 ppi for the Resolution, and click OK. Now you've got a blank image. Go to the photo of the large half-basketball, choose Select>All, then go ahead and copy-and-paste it into your blank image. Use the Move tool (V) to position it toward the bottom. You should now have two layers—the Background layer with the basketball layer on top of it.

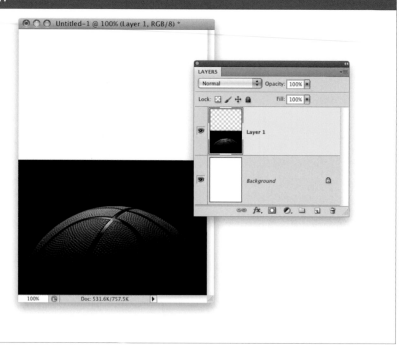

STEP 3: SELECT THE GRADIENT TOOL AND USE THE BLACK, WHITE GRADIENT

This time around we're going to blend the large half-basketball into the background but in a much easier (and non-destructive) way. If you recall, layer masks see only in black and white, and they don't care how you actually get black and white on them. So, let's try using a gradient to give us a nice, smooth blend. Select the Gradient tool from the Toolbox (or just press G). Then click on the down-facing arrow to the right of the gradient thumbnail in the Options Bar, and choose the third gradient from the left in the Gradient Picker. It's the default Black, White gradient. Also make sure you click on the Linear Gradient (leftmost) icon in the Options Bar and turn on the Reverse checkbox.

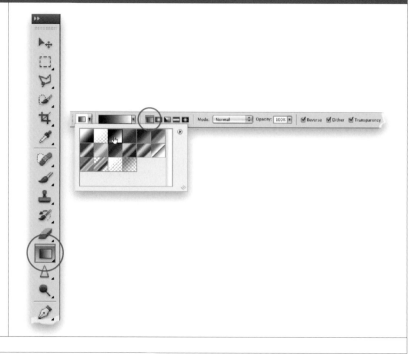

STEP 4: ADD A LAYER MASK AND CLICK-AND-DRAG ON IT TO BLEND THE TOP

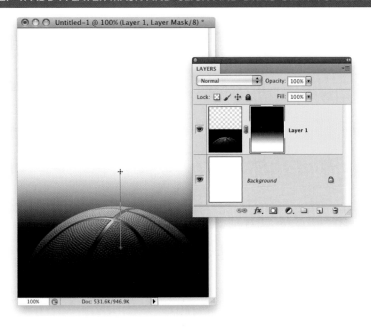

Now that you've got your gradient selected, let's use it on a layer mask. Select the large basketball layer and click on the Add Layer Mask icon to add a layer mask to it. Then, click near the bottom of the ball and drag upward to the top of it. When you release your mouse button, you'll have created a gradient on the layer mask. More than that, though, look at your image. The ball now blends nicely into the Background layer. If yours looks off, it's probably because of the way you dragged your gradient. Sometimes it takes a few tries, so feel free to drag over it again to adjust the gradient, as well as the overall blend.

STEP 5: BRING ANOTHER PHOTO INTO THE MAIN IMAGE

Now let's bring in the photo of the basketball player. Copy-and-paste it into our main collage document that we've been working on. Use the Move tool to position it in the middle. Now you should have three layers in the collage document: Background, the large basketball, and the basketball player. Go ahead and add a layer mask to this layer, as well, just like the other one.

STEP 6: USE THE GRADIENT TOOL AGAIN TO HIDE PART OF THAT PHOTO

You'll notice the photo of the basketball player totally covers up the large basketball below it. Let's use the same Black, White gradient on the basketball player's layer mask, but turn off the Reverse checkbox, and click-and-drag from the bottom to the top to fade the bottom part of the basketball player away, and reveal the large basketball below it. Once you do this, you'll be able to see part of the white Background layer, so click on it, make sure your Foreground color is set to black, and press Option-Delete (PC: Alt-Backspace) to fill it with black.

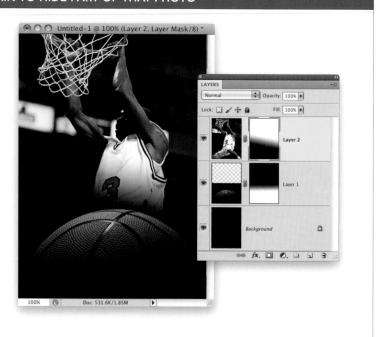

STEP 7: BRING THE LAST PHOTO INTO THE MAIN IMAGE

Copy-and-paste the last photo (the fiery basketball) into the main image. Make sure it's the topmost layer in the Layers panel. Use the Move tool to position it toward the top left of the image, over the basketball net. Now, add a layer mask to this layer.

STEP 8: USE THE BRUSH TOOL TO FADE THE PHOTO

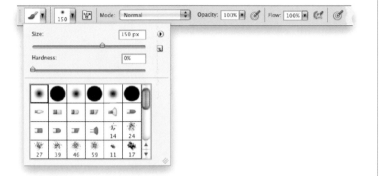

Now we need to blend the new layer into the image. We could use the Gradient tool again, but that's no fun. That's old news, right? Instead, let's try using the Brush tool because we can be a lot more precise in the areas we blend. Remember, we did this with our adjustment layer back in Chapter 3 when we had to hide the background around the mom and daughter from the Curves adjustment. So select the Brush tool (B). Click on the brush thumbnail in the Options Bar and set the Size to something fairly large, like 150 pixels. Then set the Hardness to 0% so the edges are very soft and feathered.

STEP 9: PAINT WITH BLACK ON THE LAYER MASK

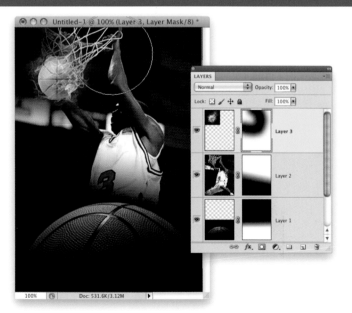

Now, click once on the layer mask thumbnail to select it. Press D, then X to set your Foreground color to black. Start painting around the basketball to hide its black background, so it fades nicely into the net. As you paint, that area of the photo will disappear. Use the Right and Left Bracket keys to change the size of your brush, if needed.

Let's say, for example, you hide an area of your photo that you didn't want to. Just switch your Foreground color to white (press the X key) and paint over it again. Wherever you paint with white, you'll start to bring back the original photo. This means you can get very creative and experiment with different degrees of blending your photos with each other.

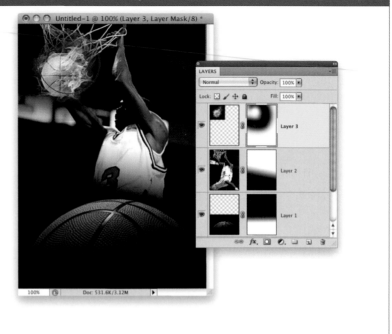

STEP 11: ADD THE FINISHING TOUCHES

Lastly, I've added the same graphic and text to finish things off.

Is it pretty much the same final image we came away with in Chapter 1? Yep. But we accomplished the same thing, with just about the same amount of work, in a non-destructive way. Now we can change the image if we ever need to. If you had erased those areas away, like we did in Chapter 1, you wouldn't have the flexibility to move and change the layers—you'd have to start all over again.

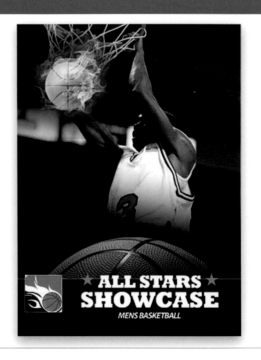

MAKING ONE LAYER FIT INTO ANOTHER

FORCING THE CONTENTS OF ONE LAYER TO FIT INSIDE THE CONTENTS OF ANOTHER LAYER

There's another masking feature that comes in really handy. It's called a clipping mask, and it's another type of mask that we use with layers. Its main purpose is letting you use a shape on one layer to mask layers above it. Clipping masks have a ton of good uses, but one great example is creating a greeting card. Plus, I'll show you a very slick little shortcut for aligning multiple layers more precisely.

STEP 1: CREATE A NEW BLANK DOCUMENT

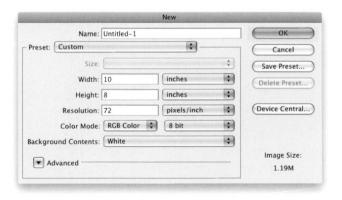

We'll kick off our greeting card by creating a brand new blank document. Click on the File menu and choose New (or just press Command-N [PC: Ctrl-N]). In the New dialog, type the size of the final image you want to create. In this example, let's create a document that is 8 inches by 10 inches at a resolution of 72 ppi. Click OK to create the new document.

STEP 2: CREATE A ROUNDED RECTANGLE SELECTION FILLED WITH BLACK ON A NEW LAYER

Select the Rectangular Marquee tool (M) and create a rectangle in the middle of the canvas. Then click the Select menu and choose Modify>Smooth. Enter 15 pixels for the Sample Radius and click OK. This creates a rounded rectangular selection. Now click on the Create a New Layer icon at the bottom of the Layers panel to create a new blank layer. Press D to set your Foreground color to black, and press Option-Delete (PC: Alt-Backspace) to fill the selection with black. Press Command-D (PC: Ctrl-D) to Deselect.

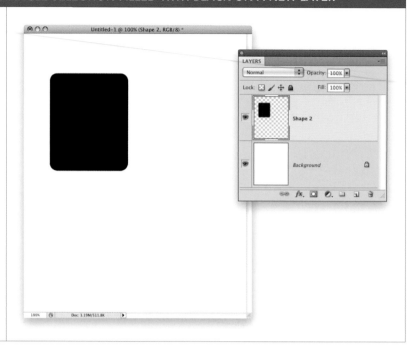

STEP 3: COPY-AND-PASTE THE PHOTO YOU WANT TO APPEAR ON THE CARD ONTO A NEW LAYER

Open the photo that you want to appear on the card. In this example, we're creating a family greeting card, so we'll use a photo of a little girl. Press Command-A (PC: Ctrl-A) to select the photo. Press Command-C (PC: Ctrl-C), then switch documents, and press Command-V (PC: Ctrl-V) to copy-and-paste the photo into the card image we just created. Make sure it's on a layer above the rectangle layer in the Layers panel.

MATT KLOSKOWSKI

STEP 4: CREATE A CLIPPING MASK TO FORCE THE GIRL TO FIT INSIDE THE ROUNDED RECTANGLE

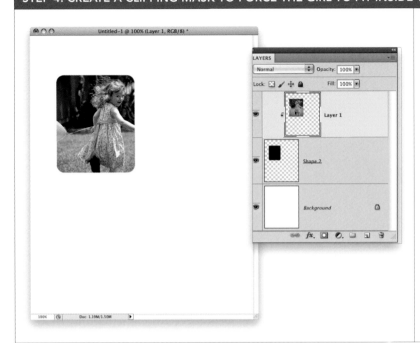

Click once on the girl layer to select it. Click the Layer menu and choose Create Clipping Mask, or just press Command-Option-G (PC: Ctrl-Alt-G). This forces the photo of the girl to only appear inside the boundaries of the layer below it. Even better, select the Move tool (V) and move the photo around. You'll see that you can move it around anywhere you want and it still only reveals itself inside that original rounded rectangle shape. In fact, you can resize it, as well. Just choose Edit>Free Transform, or press Command-T (PC: Ctrl-T), and resize or rotate it at will. You have total control, and you never have to worry about the photo extending beyond the boundaries of the layer below.

STEP 5: OKAY, SO WHAT'S REALLY GOING ON HERE?

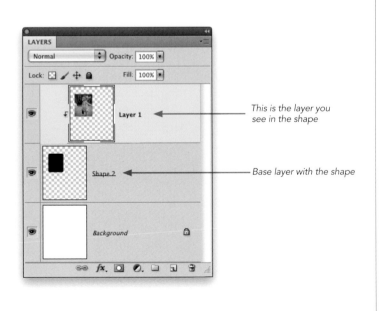

This is the layer you see in the shape

Base layer with the shape

Pretty cool, right? So, what the heck is really going on here? Think of it this way: the bottom layer (or base layer) of a clipping mask is the shape you want to see in the final image. In this case, it's taken the form of a rounded rectangle, but it doesn't always have to be that way. It could be any shape—circle, square, logo, text, etc. That base layer tells Photoshop what shape or object you want to see in the end. Everything else that appears on top of that layer is what you'll actually see in the image. It's "clipped," though, and the shape below is what's clipping it (hence the name "clipping mask").

STEP 6: DUPLICATE THE RECTANGLE AND REPOSITION IT USING SMART GUIDES

Let's finish this up. Click once on the rounded rectangle layer and press Command-J (PC: Ctrl-J) to duplicate it. Your photo will now be clipped to the duplicate, so click on the original rounded rectangle layer and use the Move tool to move it next to the other one. You'll find that moving layers around and aligning them with each other can be difficult. Smart Guides can help. Go to the View menu and choose Show>Smart Guides. Then make sure you have View>Snap turned on. As you drag the new rectangle layer around, you'll see guides pop up as you align the top of the layer with the top of another layer in the Layers panel.

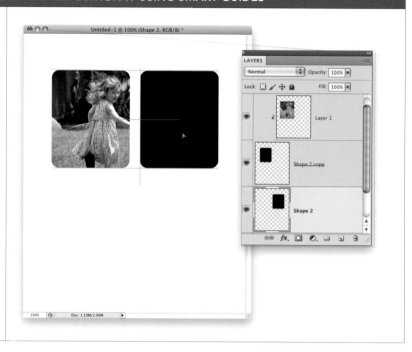

STEP 7: ADD ANOTHER PHOTO TO THE IMAGE

Go ahead and copy-and-paste another photo for this greeting card into the image. Move it above the new black rounded rectangle layer and go to Layer>Create Clipping Mask again. Repeat Step 6 and this step one more time for the last photo in the bottom left. You'll see those Smart Guides really help when positioning this one.

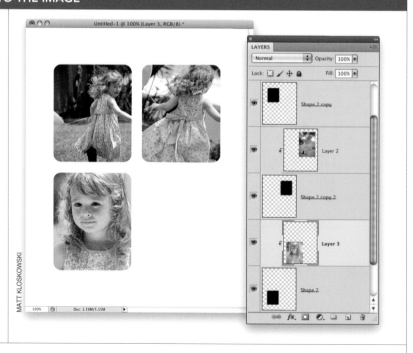

MATT KLOSKOWSKI

Make one more copy of the black rounded rectangle layer. Use the Move tool to move it into position in the bottom right. Since black doesn't really work for this photo, let's try another color. First, click on your Foreground color swatch and set the color to R: 211, G: 138, B: 152. Then grab the Paint Bucket tool (it's nested under the Gradient tool in the Toolbox). As long as the layer you want to paint on with the Paint Bucket tool is active, all you have to do is click on the object you want to fill and Photoshop will automatically fill it with the Foreground color. It won't fill anything else on the layer, though—just the rounded rectangle shape.

Add some text and graphics and you're done. In this example, I copied-and-pasted a few of the scribbles that we saw back in the beginning of Chapter 2, and changed their blend mode to Screen to drop out the black background. I added her name and the year (in the Cooper Std font), as well, to finish things off.

IDEA 1: HERE'S ANOTHER USE FOR CLIPPING MASKS: PUTTING A PHOTO INTO TEXT

Another really popular technique that clipping masks are used for is to make a photo appear inside of text. Just create a Type layer (more on that in Chapter 5) and move a photo onto a layer above it using the Move tool. Then click on the photo layer and create a clipping mask with it. Now you'll only see the photo inside of the shape of the text.

IDEA 2: CLIPPING MASKS ALSO COME IN HANDY FOR MARKETING DESIGN

Clipping masks can also be used to place a photo into any shape you can create. And you don't have to have only one shape on a layer. Here, I painted with black, using some grungy splatter brushes, on a blank layer to make my clipping mask. Then, I brought in a photo of a person's tattoo and clipped it to that mask. Add a layer with the company's logo, and you've got a cool marketing design that can be updated just by placing another photo in it.

HOW DO I...

TURN OFF OR DISABLE A LAYER MASK?

Shift-click on the layer mask thumbnail in the Layers panel. You'll see a red X appear over it. It's still there, but the layer mask is disabled. Shift-click again on it to enable it.

VIEW THE CONTENTS OF A LAYER MASK?

To see the contents of a layer mask, or see it in black-and-white mode, Option-click (PC: Alt-click) on it. Now you'll just see the mask onscreen, and you can adjust it (paint on it) there just as you normally would. Option-click on it again to get back to the normal view.

MOVE A LAYER MASK TO ANOTHER LAYER?

To move a layer mask, just click-and-drag the layer mask to another layer.

COPY A LAYER MASK TO ANOTHER LAYER?

To copy a layer mask, press-and-hold the Option (PC: Alt) key and click-and-drag the layer mask to another layer. You'll see a double-arrow cursor indicating that you're duplicating the mask and not just moving it.

DELETE A LAYER MASK?

Drag the layer mask to the Trash icon at the bottom of the Layers panel.

MOVE THE CONTENTS OF A LAYER WITHOUT MOVING THE LAYER MASK ITSELF?

To move what is actually on the layer around in your image, but leave the layer mask exactly where it is, you need to unlink the two. Click on the little chain-link icon between the layer thumbnail and the layer mask thumbnail to unlink them. Click that space again to re-link the two.

APPLY A LAYER MASK PERMANENTLY TO A LAYER?

To apply a layer mask permanently to a layer, so it actually deletes the masked areas, Right-click on the layer mask icon, and then choose Apply Layer Mask from the pop-up menu that appears.

CHAPTER FIVE

TYPE AND SHAPE LAYERS

There are two more popular categories of layers that we haven't covered yet: type layers and shape layers. While you use two different tools to create these layers, they actually have a lot in common, which is why I'm covering them together. Plus, if you've followed everything so far, then type and shape layers are a breeze. That doesn't mean they're not powerful, though. There are a lot of things we can do with these layers that you simply can't do (or would have a heck of a hard time doing) without them.

fx

CREATING TYPE LAYERS

TYPE LAYERS ARE HOW YOU GET TEXT INTO YOUR PHOTOSHOP DOCUMENTS. BUT THERE ARE LOTS OF EXTRAS, TOO

Creating text in Photoshop is simple enough. In fact, I probably wouldn't need to write much of a tutorial for that: select the Type tool, click on the canvas, then type away. There...we're done! But there's a ton of features when it comes to building images with professional-looking text and that's what we're going to cover in this tutorial. So, here's the deal: this is a type tutorial, but it's no fun to just create text for the heck of it, so I created a little project. It's a cover page for a health journal.

STEP 1: OPEN A BACKGROUND IMAGE

It's not absolutely necessary, but if you want to follow along with the same image I use in this tutorial, go ahead and open the image I provided. Sure, you could just add text to a blank document and do the tutorial just fine, but it makes more sense when it comes to putting type onto an image if you actually have somewhere to place it that looks good.

Note: I mentioned in the book's introduction that you can download the images I use here in the book. You can download them over at www.kelbytraining.com/books/layerscs5.

©ISTOCKPHOTO/IZABELA HABUR

STEP 2: SELECT THE TYPE TOOL AND CHANGE THE TYPE OPTIONS

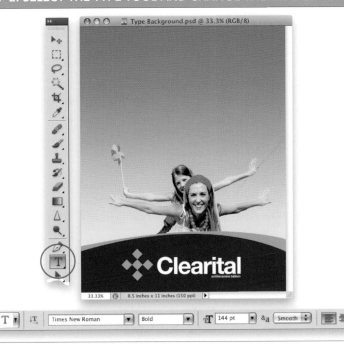

Select the Type tool (T) from the Toolbox and, from the top Options Bar, select Times New Roman for the Font Family setting. Then choose Bold for the Font Style setting and enter 144 pt for the Font Size.

STEP 3: SET YOUR FOREGROUND COLOR AND CREATE SOME TEXT

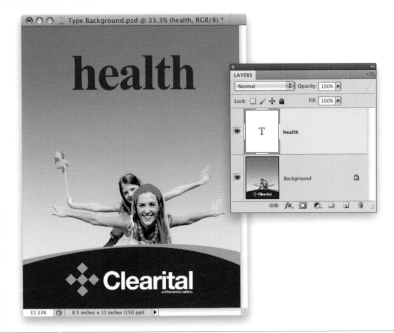

Next, click on the Foreground color swatch at the bottom of the Toolbox and, in the Color Picker, set your Foreground color to R: 42, G: 67, B: 114. Any text you create is automatically set to your Foreground color, so try to have that picked out ahead of time (you can change it later if you need to, though). Then click on the canvas and type the word *health*. When you're done, the Type tool is still active, but you can click on the Commit icon (the checkmark) in the right side of the Options Bar to commit the type, or simply click on another tool to commit your text and exit the Type tool. Here, let's click on the Move tool (V) in the Toolbox and then position the text in the top center of the image.

STEP 4: SELECT THE TYPE TOOL AGAIN AND CREATE MORE TEXT

Select the Type tool again, click on the canvas, and start typing the words *The Weekly*. Notice how the Type tool remembered your settings from the last time and created the same style of text? Same font. Same size. In fact, the text probably runs off the document.

STEP 5: SELECT THE TYPE LAYER YOU JUST CREATED AND CHANGE ITS FONT

One of the cool features about type in Photoshop is that you're never stuck with it. You can always change your mind, and that's what we'll do for the text we just created. With The Weekly type layer selected in the Layers panel, go to the Options Bar and change the Font Family setting to something really thick—I used Rockwell Extra Bold here. Then change the Font Size to 27 pt, click on the Move tool in the Toolbox, and move the text above and just to the right of the letter *h* in the word *health*.

Sometimes you'll want to edit text after you've already created it. Well that's the whole benefit of editable type—you can always change your mind. To edit your text, you've got two options: (1) double-click on the Type layer in the Layers panel to select the text and type something else, or (2) click on the text itself and drag over the specific letters you want to change to highlight them. Here, I've selected the word *Weekly* and changed it to *Daily*, and changed the point size of this whole layer to 31.

You're not stuck with the color of your text either. With The Daily type layer selected, click-and-drag over the word *Daily* to select it and then click on the Foreground color swatch in the Toolbox. In the Color Picker, change the color to a light blue color (here I used R: 197, G: 223, B: 247), and then press Command-Return (PC: Ctrl-Enter) to commit the change.

Next, let's type the word *Journal* below the word *health*. Just like before, it'll pick up the last font, size, and color you used, which is fine, but this time when you're done, select all of this new text. Then, click on the Font Family pop-up menu to show all of your fonts. You'll see a WYSIWYG (what-you-see-is-what-you-get) preview of each font installed on your computer on the right side of the menu so you can pick one visually.

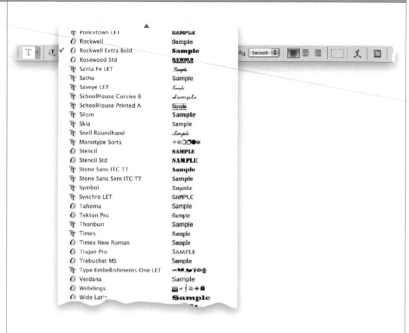

The WYSIWYG preview is neat and all, but I have to be honest, it's not my preferred way of picking fonts. First, it's small. Second, it only shows the word *Sample*, which is fine if you type the word *Sample* all the time, but chances are you don't. Here's my preferred way: Select the text and click on the Font Family name in the pop-up menu in the Options Bar (it will become highlighted). Now, are you ready for this? Just press your Up or Down Arrow key to cycle through all of the fonts and Photoshop will automatically swap out the text on your canvas with the newly selected font. This way, you can get a live preview of the font you have selected.

I've settled on the font Century Gothic for the Journal layer. I also changed the Font Size to 46 points and left the text color set to the same light blue we used for the word *Daily*. Now let's change the Journal layer to all caps. Instead of retyping, though, just click on the Window menu and choose Character. Then click on the arrow at the top right of the Character panel, and from the flyout menu, choose All Caps. It's just one word here so it would be no big deal to change it manually, but if you had more text, it could be time consuming.

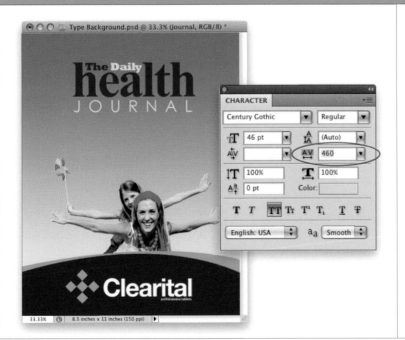

I'd also like to make the word *JOURNAL* appear as wide as the word *health*. Now, I don't want to increase the font size, I just want to spread out the amount of space between each letter. We'll call on the Character panel for this, since we just used it in Step 10. First, select the word *JOURNAL*, and then in the Character panel, go to the field with the little letters AV with a double-sided arrow under them. That's the Tracking setting. Click in the Tracking field and start hitting the Up Arrow key. You'll see the spacing between the letters start to increase. I set mine to 460 and used the Move tool (V) to position *JOURNAL* under *health*.

Go ahead and add some more text to the page, following the example here. (For *manage your allergies*, I used Monotype Corsiva set to 42 points in black.) Now, click on the top Type layer in your Layers panel and then Shift-click on the bottom Type layer to select all of the Type layers. With the Move tool, move all of the type up a bit toward the top of the image. This is going to help make a little room for what we're going to do in the next step.

The next thing I want to add is a large block of text. So far, all of the text we've created has been on one line. Now we want to add some text that spans multiple lines. You could just hit the Return (PC: Enter) key at the end of each line to go to the next one, but that's the hard way—it works, but it doesn't work well. Instead, we'll use a little trick with the Type tool to create a text block. First, select the Type tool (T) from the Toolbox, then click-and-drag to create a rectangle, just like you would with a selection tool. This creates a text box just waiting for you to type in it.

Choose the font family, style, size, and color you want and start typing (I used Myriad Pro at 13 points in white). Watch what happens as you type near the end of the line, though. As your text hits the far-right side of the text box, it will automatically wrap to the next line. You don't have to do a thing. Of course, you could always manually hit the Return (PC: Enter) key if you wanted to put a hard line break in, but the whole point of using a text box is that you don't have to.

As soon as you create a text box, you open up a whole new set of possibilities for editing. Now you can use the Paragraph panel to change your type alignment and justification. Click on the Window menu and choose Paragraph. The alignment options are near the top left of the panel and the justification options are on the top right. For this example, click on the Justify Last Left icon (the fourth icon from the right) to make your text spread evenly across the entire text box.

STEP 16: TRY TO APPLY A GRADIENT OR FILTER TO A TYPE LAYER

We're almost done, but there's one more thing I'd like to do: I want to spice up the word *health*, and a gradient is a nice way to do that. Problem is, you really can't. Try it. Select the Health layer in the Layers panel, and then select the Gradient tool (G) from the Toolbox. Position your cursor over your document and you'll see the little symbol for "no way."

STEP 17: DUPLICATE A TYPE LAYER. HIDE THE ORIGINAL, THEN RASTERIZE THE DUPLICATE

The point I'm trying to make is that your Type layers are special kinds of layers. There are certain things you can't do to them (like add filters or gradients or use a brush on them). To do these things, we need to rasterize the layer. It's easy to do, but the text will no longer be editable. With the Health layer selected, press Command-J (PC: Ctrl-J) to duplicate it. Hide the original (so we have a backup) by clicking on the Eye icon to the left of the layer thumbnail. Right-click on the duplicate and choose Rasterize Type. This turns the Type layer into a regular old layer. Now you can apply gradients and filters, but you can't change the text anymore, so there's a tradeoff.

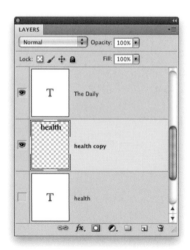

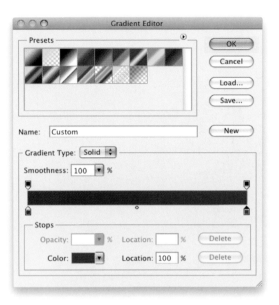

With the Gradient tool still selected, click on the gradient thumbnail in the Options Bar. This opens the Gradient Editor. Now let's create a gradient that starts on the left with a dark blue, then goes to a lighter blue. First, double-click on the Color Stop on the bottom left of the Gradient Bar. From the Color Picker, choose a blue color (I chose R: 40, G: 63, B: 107). Then, click on the bottom-right Color Stop and choose a lighter blue (R: 54, G: 84, B: 143).

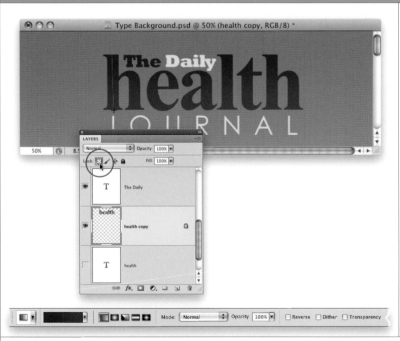

In the Options Bar, click on the Linear Gradient icon (the first icon to the right of the gradient thumbnail). We'll click-and-drag the gradient from top to bottom on the word *health*. However, there's one little trick: If we just click-and-drag on this layer, it'll fill the whole layer. So, click on the Lock Transparent Pixels icon at the top left of the Layers panel, as shown here. This locks everything that is transparent. Now click-and-drag from the top of the word *health* to the bottom to add the gradient.

ALL ABOUT SHAPE LAYERS

ADD A WHOLE NEW DIMENSION TO YOUR IMAGES WITH PHOTOSHOP'S SHAPE LAYERS

Photoshop's Shape layers are one of those overlooked areas that are really very powerful. What if you need to create a shape but you just can't do it with any of the selection tools? Shape tools can help. If you want to create a Web icon or button, then you'll love Shape layers. If you need to go beyond simple shapes and create your own complex ones, then Shape layers are the place to turn. You can even save them as a preset so you can use them again later. There are literally thousands of possibilities. If you've never given shapes in Photoshop the time of day, then check out this tutorial and learn how to start putting them to work for you.

STEP 1: CREATE A NEW BLANK DOCUMENT

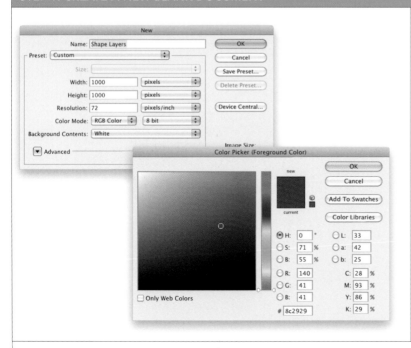

Start out by creating a new blank document by choosing File>New. Enter 1000x1000 pixels for the width and height and 72 ppi for the resolution. Name your new document and click OK. Click on the Foreground color swatch at the bottom of the Toolbox, and in the Color Picker, set your Foreground color to R: 140, G: 41, B: 41. Click OK, and then press Option-Delete (PC: Alt-Backspace) to fill the Background layer with the red Foreground color.

Now select the Rectangle tool (U) from the Toolbox. Notice that this isn't the Rectangular Marquee tool—it's the Rectangle tool and it's located further down in the Toolbox. If you click-and-hold on it in the Toolbox, you'll see a pop-up menu with a few other shapes, as well, but we just want the Rectangle tool for now. Take a look in the left of the Options Bar and you will see there are three little icons. The first one is the Shape Layers icon, so make sure you click on it to select it. That ensures that we create a Shape layer.

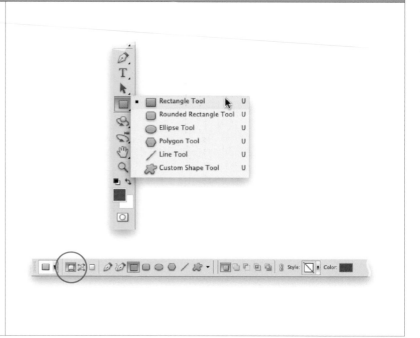

STEP 3: DRAW A RECTANGLE ON THE BOTTOM OF THE CANVAS

Press D to set your Foreground color to black and then click-and-drag out a rectangle at the bottom of the canvas with the Rectangle tool. If you don't position it correctly the first time, just press-and-hold the Spacebar to move it around as you click-and-drag.

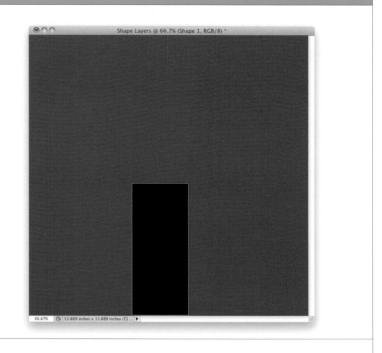

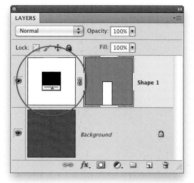

After you create the shape, you'll notice a new layer appear in the Layers panel. This layer should look pretty different from anything that we've seen before this chapter—it's a Shape layer. Shape layers are cool for a few reasons—one of them being, you can change its color by simply double-clicking on the layer thumbnail (the one on the left of the layer). Try it: double-click on the Shape layer thumbnail and try choosing different colors. We're going to leave ours black, though, so click Cancel in the Color Picker when you're done.

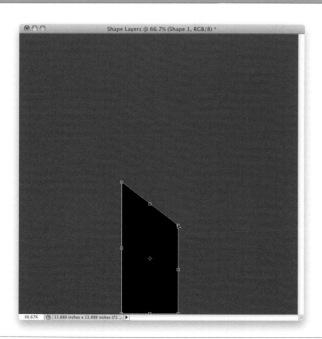

A Shape layer is a lot like other layers in that it can be resized and transformed. Go to Edit>Free Transform (or just press Command-T [PC: Ctrl-T]), then press-and-hold the Command (PC: Ctrl) key, and click on the top-right corner point. Drag it downward and you'll see how you can change the overall shape of the layer. Press Return (PC: Enter) when you're done to commit the transformation and exit Free Transform.

STEP 6: ADD TO THE SHAPE

Another cool feature of Shape layers is that you're not stuck with the shape once you create it. There are lots of ways to change them. We used Edit>Free Transform, but there's something even better: With the Rectangle tool, in the Options Bar, click on the Add to Shape Area icon (shown circled in red). You'll see a little plus sign icon at the bottom right of your cursor. Click-and-drag another rectangle that intersects with the top right of the first one you created (press-and-hold the Spacebar while clicking-and-dragging to move the rectangle as you create it). Now, take a look over at the Shape layer thumbnail in the Layers panel. You've just added to that shape without creating another Shape layer.

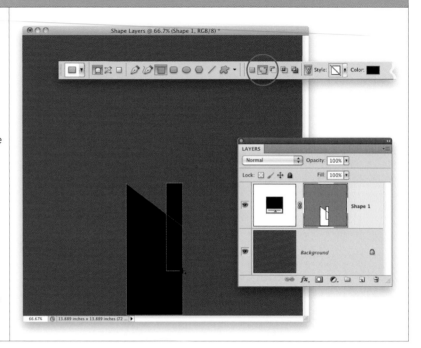

STEP 7: SUBTRACT FROM THE SHAPE

This time we'll remove some of the shape. So, click on the Subtract from Shape Area icon up in the Options Bar (it's shown circled in red) and click-and-drag a small rectangle inside the smaller one you just created (just press-and-hold the Spacebar to move it around as you click-and-drag). When you release your mouse button, you'll see that area is removed from the overall shape.

TIP: When working on a Shape layer, be sure the shape is selected by making sure the gray thumbnail (a vector mask) to the right of the Shape layer thumbnail is active—you'll know when you see an outline around the thumbnail, and around the shape on your canvas.

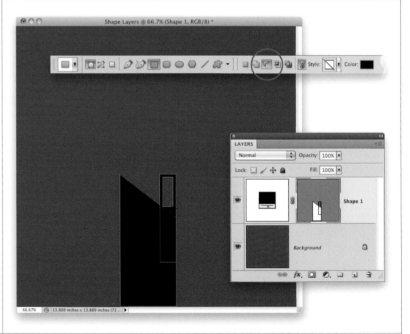

STEP 8: CREATE A FEW MORE SHAPES

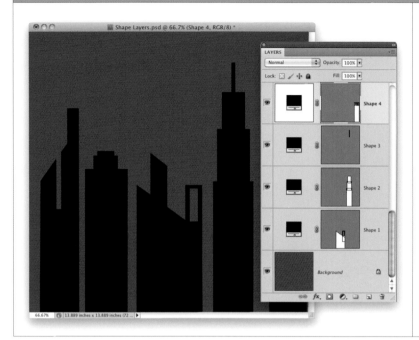

Repeat Steps 3–7 a few more times to create some random, city-building-like shapes. These are going to be a background for our final image.

STEP 9: GROUP THEM TOGETHER. RESIZE. REDUCE THE OPACITY

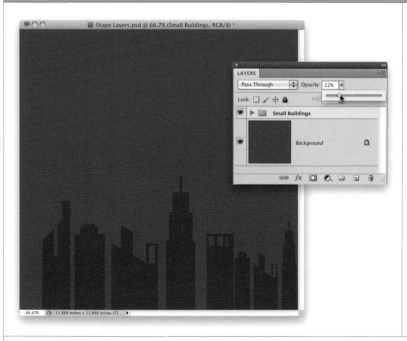

Let's tidy up the Layers panel by grouping these layers together. Click on the bottom-most Shape layer in the Layers panel and then Shift-click on the top one to select all of the building shapes. Then go to Layer>Group Layers to put them all into a group. Double-click on the group's name in the Layers panel and rename this building group, so that you know what's inside this group. Now, you can resize them (using Edit>Free Transform) and move them around as one group, like I did here. I also lowered the Opacity setting to 22% (as shown here).

Rectangles aren't the only kind of shape you can create. There are several others and each has its own set of options. Select the Polygon tool in the Options Bar (it's circled here in red) and then click on the small down-facing arrow to the right of the shapes to bring up the tool's options (shown here). Turn on the Smooth Corners, Star, and Smooth Indents checkboxes, then enter 100 in the Sides field (to the right of the arrow in the Options Bar). Click on the Color swatch in the right of the Options Bar and set your Foreground color to yellow, then click-and-drag to create a new Shape layer. You'll see it looks like a sun with rays coming out from it. Use the Move tool (V) to move it off into the bottom-left corner.

Let's make the sun's rays look a little better. Press-and-hold the Option key and then click on the Add Layer Mask icon at the bottom of the Layers panel. Get the Gradient tool (G) from the Toolbox, then click on the down-facing arrow to the right of the gradient thumbnail in the Options Bar. Choose the Foreground to Background gradient (as shown here), and click on the Radial Gradient icon to the right of the gradient thumbnail. Click-and-drag from the bottom-left corner of the image outward to reveal the sun shape layer underneath the black layer mask. Now, just click on the sun's shape layer thumbnail (the one on the right in the layer) to deactivate it and see the effect of the gradient.

STEP 12: OPEN AN IMAGE. SELECT IT AND TURN THE SELECTION INTO A PATH

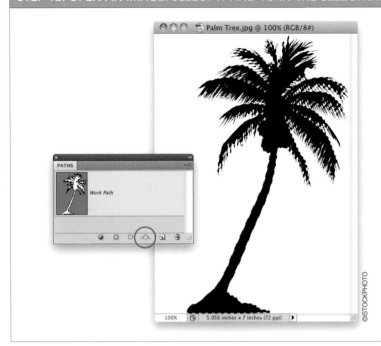

So far, we've been using shapes that come with Photoshop, but you can also make and use your own. Open the image of this black palm tree. Select the Magic Wand tool from the Toolbox (or press Shift-W until you have it) and click on the black palm tree to select it (Shift-click on any missed areas to add to the selection). Before we can turn this into a custom shape, though, we need to turn it into a path first. So, click the Window menu and choose Paths to open the Paths panel. Then click the Make Work Path from Selection icon at the bottom of the Paths panel (circled here). This turns the selection into a path, which is the first step in making a custom shape.

STEP 13: CLICK THE EDIT MENU AND DEFINE A CUSTOM SHAPE FROM THE PALM TREE

Now that you have a path created, click the Edit menu and choose Define Custom Shape. Enter a descriptive name in the Shape Name dialog (something like "Palm Tree") and click OK. Now you've got a custom shape ready to use in any image, not just this one.

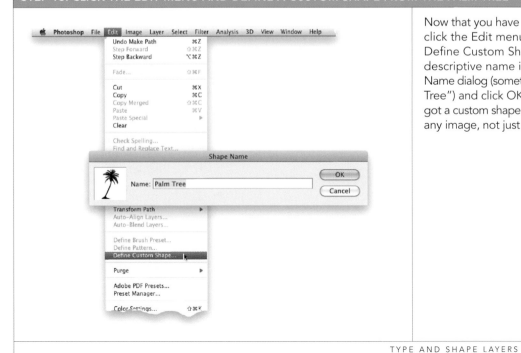

STEP 14: USE YOUR NEW CUSTOM SHAPE

Go back to the Shape tools, but this time click on the Custom Shape tool in the Options Bar (the last one on the right). Click on the Shape thumbnail, scroll to the bottom of the Shape Picker, and you'll see the new palm tree shape there. Click on it and, with your Foreground color set to black, go ahead and create a palm tree shape layer on the image (remember to press-and-hold the Spacebar to position the shape as you create it).

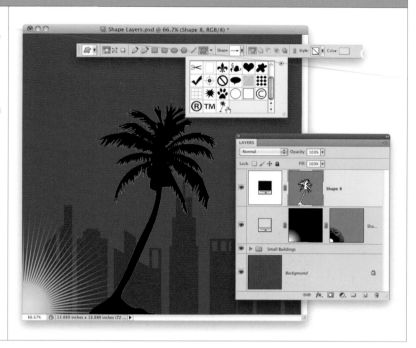

STEP 15: ADD ANOTHER SHAPE LAYER AND FLIP IT

Create a smaller palm tree shape layer and then go to the Edit menu and under Transform Path, choose Flip Horizontal. Now, use the Move tool to reposition this palm tree shape, so it appears like you see here.

Next, we'll turn a regular photo into a custom shape, but first we need adjust it so that it's one solid color, because that's all a custom shape can work with. So, open the photo (you can download the same photo of the buildings I'm using here from the books' companion website mentioned in the introduction) and go to Image>Adjustments>Threshold. Enter 100 as the Threshold Level amount and click OK.

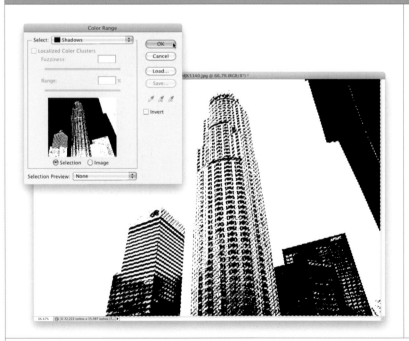

Now, let's turn the buildings photo into a custom shape, just like we did with the palm tree. But, we'll do something different here to make our selection. First, choose Select>Color Range. From the Select pop-up menu at the top, choose Shadows, and then click OK to select the blacks in the photo.

Next, do the same thing you did to turn the palm tree into a Shape layer: Go to the Paths panel and click on the Make Work Path from Selection icon at the bottom of the panel. This turns the selection into a path. Then go to the Edit menu and choose Define Custom Shape, give it a name, and click OK. Finally, choose this new shape from the Custom Shape tool's Shape Picker in the Options Bar, and use it to make a new Shape layer for our image. Use Free Transform (Command-T [PC: Ctrl-T]) to resize it, as needed. Click on the Small Buildings group in the Layers panel and use Free Transform to make them a little smaller, then add some text to finish it off.

The last thing I want to do is really just a quick demonstration to show you one last really cool feature of Shape layers (and Type layers, for that matter). Click the Image menu and choose Image Size. Change the Document Size to something really big—like five times what the size is now—then click OK. If you look at the newly sized image, you'll see the edges are still perfectly crisp and no quality was lost on any Shape or Type layer. That's because Shape and Type layers are vector layers, and that's just a techie way of saying they aren't pixels. You can always resize them however you want without losing any quality.

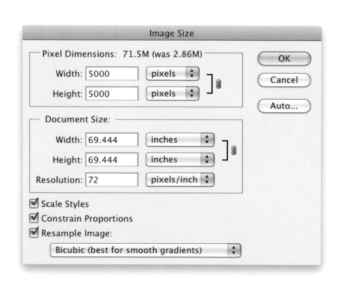

HOW DO I...

QUICKLY SELECT MY TEXT?

Double-click on the Type layer thumbnail (the thing with the T on it) in the Layers panel. That selects all of the type on that Type layer.

QUICKLY SEE WHAT DIFFERENT FONT FAMILIES WILL LOOK LIKE ON MY TEXT?

First, double-click the Type layer thumbnail to select your text. Then click once in the Font Family pop-up menu. Use your Up and Down Arrow keys to cycle up or down your font list and preview onscreen what a different font will look like. If you don't like any of them, just press the Esc key.

HIDE THE HIGHLIGHT AROUND MY TEXT WHEN I'M TRYING TO SEE WHAT A DIFFERENT FONT LOOKS LIKE?

Press Command-H (PC: Ctrl-H). Make sure you remember you did it, though, and press it again to see the highlight later.

CHANGE THE SIZE OF THE FONT SAMPLE PREVIEW IN THE FONT FAMILY POP-UP MENU?

Yep, that little font preview that says *Sample* is resizable. If you want to make it larger, go to Photoshop's preferences (Photoshop>Preferences>Type on a Mac or Edit>Preferences>Type on a PC). At the bottom of the Type options section, change the Font Preview Size setting to something larger and click OK.

MAKE MY FONT SIZE LARGER OR SMALLER WITHOUT GOING TO THE FONT SIZE SETTING IN THE OPTIONS BAR?

Press Command-Shift-> (PC: Ctrl-Shift->) to make your font size larger or press Command-Shift-< (PC: Ctrl-Shift-<) to make it smaller.

DUPLICATE A TYPE LAYER?

Press Command-J (PC: Ctrl-J), just like you would any other layer.

OPEN THE CHARACTER PANEL?

The long way is to click the Window menu and choose Character. The quick way is to press Command-T (PC: Ctrl-T). You've got to have some text selected first, though, to use the shortcut. Otherwise that shortcut will take you into Free Transform mode.

OPEN THE PARAGRAPH PANEL?

Choose Window>Paragraph.

CHAPTER SIX

ENHANCING PHOTOS WITH LAYERS

This chapter is all about enhancing digital photography. It's about making the photos that you see on your computer (and eventually print out) look like they did when you were there taking the photo. Throughout this chapter, I think you'll see one common theme (yes, besides techniques to enhance your photography), and that is simplicity. These techniques don't take 50 layers to achieve. In fact, you won't win any prizes for using a bunch of layers to enhance your photos. For me, it's quite the opposite. The fewer layers I use, the easier it is to work, and the more I get done.

fx

COMBINING MULTIPLE EXPOSURES

ONE OF THE HOTTEST THINGS TO DO RIGHT NOW IN PHOTOGRAPHY IS TO COMBINE TWO EXPOSURES INTO ONE

If you've ever taken a photo only to find the sky is totally blown out but the rest of the photo looks fine, then this tutorial is for you. Here's why: When you take a photo that has a bright sky in it, you have to make a choice. Do you want to set your camera to expose for the sky so the sky looks good, or do you want to set it to expose for the foreground area or subject so that looks good? Many times, choosing one will make the other look bad. If you expose for the sky, then the foreground is typically very dark. If you expose for the foreground, then the sky will probably be too bright and lose all of the detail. Well, with a little planning ahead there's a workaround: multiple exposures. You can take one photo to expose for the sky and another one to expose for the foreground. Then, with layers and layer masks, there's a simple way to combine both and get the best of both worlds.

STEP 1: OPEN THE TWO PHOTOS THAT YOU'D LIKE TO COMBINE

Start out by opening the two photos that you'd like to combine. In this example, I took two photos of the same scene. First off, this depends heavily on shooting on a tripod, since you're going to overlay these two photos and they need to match up. Next, I took the first photo with the purpose of making sure the sky looked good. As you can see, it does, but the foreground is way too dark. So, I left the tripod right where it was and took another photo and changed the exposure to make sure the foreground looked good. In doing that, you can see the sky is pretty blown out and lacking the nice detail and color that it really had.

MATT KLOSKOWSKI

MATT KLOSKOWSKI

STEP 2: BRING THE PHOTO WITH THE BAD SKY INTO THE PHOTO OF THE GOOD SKY

Copy-and-paste the photo that has the bad, blown-out sky into the other photo (the one with the good sky) by first clicking on the bad sky photo and pressing Command-A (PC: Ctrl-A) to select the entire image. Press Command-C (PC: Ctrl-C) to copy it, then click on the image with the good sky and press Command-V (PC: Ctrl-V) to paste the other photo into it. Now you should have both exposures in the same document, and it should have two layers in it. However, all you should see on the canvas is the photo that has the bad, bright sky.

STEP 3: ADD A LAYER MASK TO THE TOP LAYER

Click once on the top layer to make sure it is selected, and click on the Add Layer Mask icon at the bottom of the Layers panel to add a layer mask to it. Then, use the Quick Selection tool (W) to make a selection of the sky and clouds.

Note: I know I keep reminding you, but hey, I'm a nag. Seriously, I just want to make sure that if you happen to jump to this section of the book (without reading the rest) that you realize I created a basic selection tutorial video to accompany this book over at www.kelby-training.com/books/layerscs5.

STEP 4: FILL THE SELECTION WITH BLACK ON THE MASK TO REVEAL THE PROPERLY EXPOSED SKY

Make sure the layer mask is selected (you'll see little black frame corners around its thumbnail in the Layers panel). Choose Edit>Fill, then set the Use pop-up menu to Black and click OK (or press X to switch you Foreground color to black and press Option-Delete [PC: Alt-Backspace]) to fill the selection with black. Then press Command-D (PC: Ctrl-D) to remove the selection. This hides the bright sky and reveals the darker sky from the layer below.

TIP: Don't forget that you can also use the Brush tool (set to black or white) to paint on the mask and fine tune any edges.

STEP 5: REDUCE THE DENSITY OF THE MASK IN THE MASKS PANEL

Sometimes the sky can look a little too dark, depending on the exposure of the two photos. That's where the Masks panel comes in handy. Click on the layer mask thumbnail and go to Window>Masks to see the Masks panel. Then, reduce the Density setting. It's like an Opacity setting for a layer mask. Reducing it will start to bring back some of the bright sky that we just hid.

fx

PAINTING WITH LIGHT

THIS IS ONE OF THE HOTTEST WAYS TO IMPROVE YOUR PHOTOS AND REALLY DRAW ATTENTION TO THE SUBJECT

Every time I teach this technique, I get folks that ask me to do more. Here's why it's so cool, though: There really isn't more. What you see is what you get. It's simple, effective, and to the point. That's why I use it so much. One extra layer and I'm done. I think you'll agree—simple is better.

STEP 1: OPEN A PHOTO WHERE THE SUBJECT NEEDS MORE FOCUS

MATT KLOSKOWSKI

Start out by opening a photo where the subject needs to stand out more. Here's a photo I took in Dubai while walking around a market. The gentleman had a great smile and, even though he was working, he posed quickly for a photo. Problem is, I think his face is a little too dark compared to the rest of the photo.

STEP 2: ADD A CURVES ADJUSTMENT LAYER, THEN HIDE IT BY FILLING IT WITH BLACK

Now, go to the Adjustments panel and click on the Curves icon to add a Curves adjustment layer. Click on the middle of the curve to add a point, and drag it upward to lighten the entire photo. Don't go too crazy at this point. You can always come back later and tweak it if you need to. One more thing: Press Command-I (PC: Ctrl-I) to invert the white layer mask and turn it to black to hide the Curves adjustment for now.

TIP: You can also click the Invert button in the Masks panel to change the layer mask from white to black.

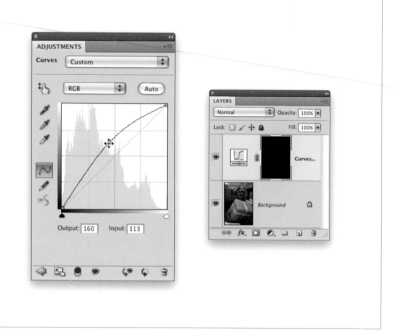

STEP 3: PAINT WITH A LOW-OPACITY, WHITE BRUSH OVER KEY PARTS OF THE PHOTO

Select the Brush tool from the Toolbox, or just press B. Click on the brush thumbnail in the Options Bar, and choose a medium-sized, soft-edged brush from the Brush Picker. Then set the brush's Opacity to 30% in the Options Bar. Press D to set your Foreground color to white (the default Foreground and Background colors are reversed on an adjustment layer) and start painting on the areas you want to add some extra light to. See? The "Painting with Light" title of the tutorial is starting to make sense now, right?

STEP 4: BUILD THE LIGHTING EFFECT BY PAINTING MULTIPLE BRUSH STROKES

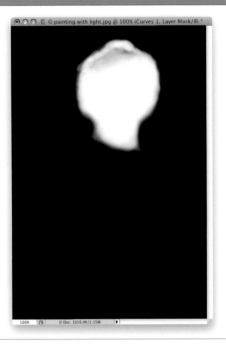

In the previous step, we set the brush opacity to 30%. That's because you want to be subtle here. You don't want your photo to look like it was lit in a fake way. If you need to add more light to specific areas, then just paint a stroke, release your mouse button, and click to paint again over it. You'll build up the effect and make those brush strokes heavier each time, which, in turn, will add more light to the areas you brush over. Just make sure to reset the opacity when you're done. Also, if you want to see your mask to see how you're doing, then Option-click (PC: Alt-click) on it. You'll see the black-and-white version. Just Option-click again to see your image again.

STEP 5: TWEAK THE CURVES ADJUSTMENT LAYER TO ADD MORE OR LESS LIGHT

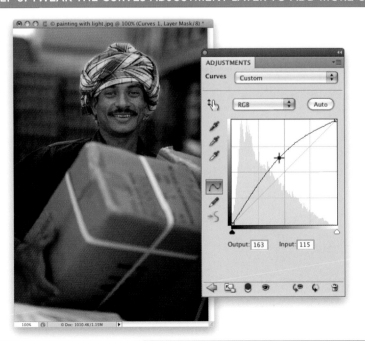

What's really cool about this lighting effect is that you can adjust it after the fact. Just click on the Curves adjustment layer thumbnail in the Layers panel to open the Curves adjustment in the Adjustments panel again. Then click-and-drag the curve upward for more light or downward for less light. All that and it just took one layer. You gotta love this stuff!

DODGING AND BURNING DONE RIGHT

WHEN YOU WANT TO DRAW ATTENTION TO PARTS OF YOUR PHOTO (OR TAKE IT AWAY),
THIS TECHNIQUE COMES IN REALLY HANDY

Dodging and burning have their roots in the film days, and involve the selective lightening and darkening of parts of a photo. Because of that, there are Dodge and Burn tools in Photoshop that work the same way they used to in the darkroom. Adobe even improved them in Photoshop CS4, but their effect is still very much a permanent and destructive one. That said, I love using the concept of dodging and burning to really lead a person through a photo by lightening areas I want them to focus on and darkening parts of the photo that I don't. With this technique, you can do just that without any of the permanent effects.

STEP 1: OPEN A PHOTO THAT NEEDS SOME DODGING AND BURNING

Open a photo that looks kind of blah. I know, what kind of photo is blah, anyway? You'll know it when you see it. It's a photo that is worth keeping, but it just lacks that punch to take it to the next level. In the photo I'm using here, everything seems to blend together. Nothing really stands out. In fact, the water at the bottom of the photo is one of the brightest and largest parts of the photo, so it's drawing all of my attention.

MATT KLOSKOWSKI

STEP 2: ADD A NEW LAYER AND FILL IT WITH 50% GRAY

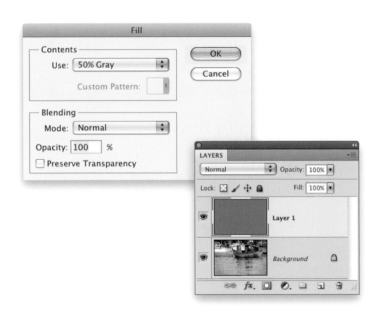

Click on the Create a New Layer icon at the bottom of the Layers panel to add a new, blank layer on top of the Background layer. Then, click the Edit menu and choose Fill. For the Use setting, select 50% Gray from the pop-up menu, and click OK.

STEP 3: CHANGE THE BLEND MODE TO OVERLAY. NOTICE HOW THIS MAKES THE GRAY TRANSPARENT

Change the blend mode of the gray layer you just made to Overlay. The Overlay blend mode hides everything that is 50% gray. This makes it appear that the gray layer is actually transparent. Go ahead, try clicking on the Eye icon next to the layer thumbnail to hide and show the layer. The image looks the same whether it's hidden or not.

TIP: You can also press Command-Shift-N (PC: Ctrl-Shift-N) to create the new layer and open the New Layer dialog. There you can change the blend mode to Overlay and fill it with 50% gray, all in one shot.

STEP 4: SELECT THE BRUSH TOOL AND SET THE OPACITY OF THE BRUSH TO 20%

Now select the Brush tool (B) from the Toolbox. Choose a medium-sized, soft-edged brush—one that is large enough to paint inside most areas that you want to dodge and burn, but not so large that you'll be painting everything. Then set the Opacity of the brush to 20% in the Options Bar.

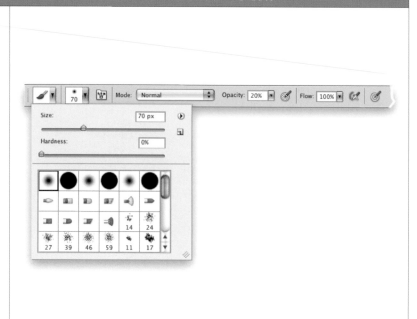

STEP 5: PAINT WITH WHITE TO SIMULATE DODGING

Click once on the gray layer to select it. Set your Foreground color to white by pressing D (for Default), then X (to swap). Now, start painting on areas in the photo that you want to dodge, or lighten. Since you're painting with a low-opacity brush, you can release the mouse button and click again to simulate multiple strokes of a brush. That'll intensify the effect and lighten the area even more. Look for key areas in the photo that you want to stand out. In this example, I'm painting over the boat in the middle, and even the ones on the far-right side.

STEP 6: PAINT WITH BLACK TO SIMULATE BURNING

Now press X (to swap your Foreground and Background colors) to set black as the Foreground color. Paint in the areas that you want to burn, or darken. This is good around areas that you don't really want to draw people's attention to. In this case, I burned in the water on the bottom, and even on the left and right sides. I also painted on the top of the photo to darken the trees a little. It has the effect of deepening the color in them, as well. Don't forget to make your brush smaller so you can paint those smaller, more detailed areas.

TIP: Use the Left Bracket ([) key to quickly make your brush smaller.

STEP 7: PAINT WITH 50% GRAY TO GET BACK TO YOUR ORIGINAL

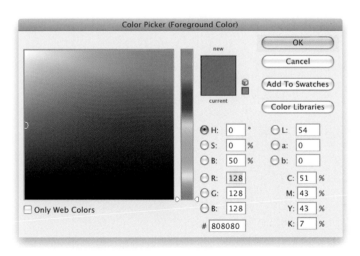

Continue painting with black or white to simulate dodging and burning. Since you're doing it all on the gray layer, nothing is destructive. Setting the brush to a low opacity gives you a nice way to creatively build the effect in areas that really need it, too. Oh yeah, if you happen to dodge or burn an area that you didn't want to, just click on your Foreground color swatch in the Toolbox, set its color to 50% gray (the color of the layer) and paint over the area. The color values are R: 128, G: 128, B: 128. That'll neutralize the effect and hide all changes, since gray appears transparent anyway. Reset your brush opacity when you're done here.

PSUEDO-HDR EFFECT

USING LAYERS, YOU CAN CREATE A FAKE HDR EFFECT IN CERTAIN AREAS OF A PHOTO

HDR photography is hot these days. It basically involves shooting several varying exposures of the same photo and then merging them all together using HDR software (like Photoshop CS5's Merge to HDR Pro). But what if you didn't take multiple photos, and only have one? Well, CS5 has a single-image adjustment called HDR Toning. With a few sliders and a couple of layers, you can still come pretty darn close to that HDR look, and give your photos a very cool finishing effect.

STEP 1: OPEN A PHOTO THAT WOULD LOOK GOOD WITH A GRUNGY EFFECT ON IT

The first step is knowing what type of photo this technique looks good on—it's got to have a certain look to it. In fact, this is a lot like the soft focus effect in this chapter, but in reverse. While the soft focus effect works best on pleasant family photos, photos of children, and just overall photos of a "soft" nature, this one does not. This technique gives a very harsh, grungy feel to a photo.

MATT KLOSKOWSKI

STEP 2: APPLY THE HDR TONING ADJUSTMENT TO THE PHOTO

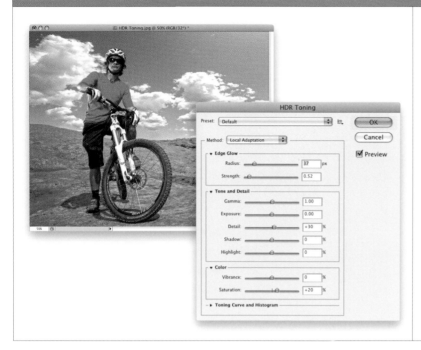

Since this is a fake HDR effect, we'll use the adjustment for it instead of the full-blown HDR Pro dialog that comes with CS5. However, it doesn't come as an adjustment layer, so you'll have to head to the Image>Adjustments menu and select HDR Toning. There's another catch to this adjustment: it doesn't work with multiple layers. If you try to run it on a document with more than one layer, it makes you flatten the image. Yeah, I know it's lame, but we'll work around that in just a minute.

STEP 3: ADJUST THE SETTINGS TO REALLY GRUNGIFY YOUR PHOTO

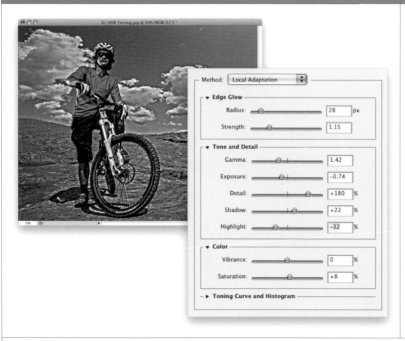

The next part is fun. Just adjust the settings to grungify the heck out of your photo (and before you ask, yes, grungify is most certainly a word, because I read it on the Internet, which means it's got to be true). Anyway, I usually find a high Detail setting works, as well as cranking up the Strength and Gamma sliders. Don't worry if it negatively affects certain parts of the photo (like skin). We'll use layers to help that next. When you're done, click OK.

grungify (grunj ə fī´) v. To make something grungy.

As you can see, the adjustment makes skin and some other areas of the photo look pretty bad. Now, we need to deal with the fact that we can't apply the HDR Toning adjustment on a multi-layered document. If we could, we would have just duplicated the layer before we applied it so we could do our masking now. Instead, we'll need to trick Photoshop for a second. First, choose Select>All and then Edit>Copy to copy this version of the image.

Now, let's undo until we get back to our original. Choose Edit>Step Backward, or press Command-Option-Z (PC: Ctrl-Alt-Z), until you're back to the original photo right before you applied the HDR Toning adjustment to it.

STEP 6: PASTE THE COPIED LAYER ON TOP OF THE ORIGINAL

Choose Edit>Paste and paste in the HDR-toned version of your photo. Remember, you just copied it a couple steps ago. Even though you stepped back to your original photo, that copied version still exists in Photoshop's memory, so when you paste it, you'll see two layers in the Layers panel—the original and the HDR-toned version.

STEP 7: ADD A BLACK LAYER MASK AND PAINT THE HDR EFFECT IN WHERE IT FITS BEST

Finally, we'll remove the HDR effects from the areas where it doesn't look good in the photo. Click on the top layer in the Layers panel to select the adjusted version. Just like we've done with many of the effects in this chapter, click on the Add Layer Mask icon at the bottom of the Layers panel to add a layer mask. Then, click the Invert button in the Masks panel to turn the mask black and hide the HDR-toned version. Set your Foreground color to white and use the Brush tool (B) to paint the effect back in the areas that need it. The effect looks great on the shirt and any clothes. It also looks cool on the tire here, so I'll paint on those areas.

REPLACING A SKY

BECAUSE SOMETIMES IT JUST HAS TO BE DONE

If you're reading this, then you're at a crossroads in your Photoshop career. See, some people will see the name of this tutorial and skip right past it, because they think it's simply not right. Unethical even. Why? Because some think of it as cheating. So, you need to make a choice. Is it okay to replace a sky in Photoshop? I think so. If I've traveled thousands of miles to shoot a beautiful location and the weather just doesn't cooperate (as you'll see in the photo below), then I feel it's my right (no, my duty!) to make the photo the way I had hoped it would turn out. If I were a photojournalist, then of course I wouldn't do something like this. But, I'm not. Heck, in addition to being a professional photographer, I'm a Photoshop Guy, so it's almost expected of me, right? Hopefully, by now, you can feel the tongue-in-cheek vibe of this introduction. I'm writing it with a smile on my face. The main idea here is that some of you won't feel this is "fair game" for your photos. No sweat! Don't do it. But a lot of you will (it's a very popular request, which is why it's in the book). So have at it, and don't feel the slightest bit guilty about it.

STEP 1: OPEN A PHOTO THAT COULD USE A NEW SKY. OPEN ANOTHER PHOTO OF A GOOD SKY

Here's where I make my case for this example: I taught a landscape photography/Photoshop workshop about a year ago. It was in an area of Washington state that I'd been wanting to visit for years—the Palouse region. It's got these beautiful, picturesque, rolling green hills with old barns and (usually) puffy clouds in the sky. Except when I went there. We had perfectly clear blue skies for the entire weekend. (I guess it could have rained, so I can't be that upset, right?) It did allow me to capture a great sunrise photo with nice light. It just has a blah layer of clouds off in the distance, though. For me, I want the pretty clouds. So, I'm going to use another photo of mine with nice clouds to make it happen.

MATT KLOSKOWSKI

STEP 2: MAKE SURE THE "FAKE" SKY PHOTO WILL WORK

Here's the deal: In order to really pull this off (and not give Photoshop a bad name), you have to make sure you pick the right "fake" cloud photo. That's why I'm always taking pictures of pretty clouds from different angles. You never know when you're going to need them. In the Palouse photo, the sun was rising from the left side, so that's my light source. For the cloud photo, I had to make sure I picked one where the sun was in just about the same position. If not, things simply wouldn't look right. Most people's minds won't be able to pinpoint what's wrong, but they'll know something just doesn't fit. Then they'll ask you the dreaded question, "Did you Photoshop this?"

STEP 3: COPY THE CLOUD PHOTO

To start, click on the photo with the nice clouds. Then, choose Select>All, or press Command-A (PC: Ctrl-A), to select the entire image. Now, choose Edit>Copy, or press Command-C (PC: Ctrl-C), to copy the photo.

STEP 4: MAKE A SELECTION OF THE BLAH SKY AND PASTE THE CLOUDS INTO IT

Switch over to the photo with the nice foreground. Use the Quick Selection tool (W) to make a rough selection of the sky. Then, go to Edit>Paste Special>Paste Into. This pastes the photo of the nice sky into our other photo, and automatically creates a mask based on the selection we just made. So, now you'll only see the good sky photo at the top.

TIP: If your selection needs improvement, click on the layer mask thumbnail, then go to the Masks panel and press the Mask Edge button to adjust it. We covered the Masks panel in more detail in Chapter 4.

STEP 5: TRANSFORM AND ADJUST THE GOOD SKY, SO IT FITS INTO OUR BLAH SKY

Lastly, choose Edit>Free Transform and resize or move the sky, so it fits nicely into our photo. Sometimes it still won't fit perfectly, though. You can see in the previous step that the trees from the cloud photo showed through. If this happens, click on the Eye icon next to the bottom layer, so only the nice sky on the top layer is showing. Then, use the Spot Healing Brush (J), with the Content-Aware option turned on in the Options Bar, to paint over the trees to remove them.

AUTO-ALIGNING LAYERS FOR GROUP PHOTOS

SOMETIMES EVERYONE ISN'T LOOKING AT THE CAMERA

There's a little known feature under the Edit menu called Auto-Align Layers. It comes in handy if you've ever taken a photo that has more than one person in it, and you later realize that not everyone was looking at the camera or someone had their eyes closed. Well, with Photoshop we can, of course, use multiple photos to get the best of each one and bring them together into one image. But trying to line each photo up manually can be tricky, which is where this Auto-Align Layers feature steps in.

STEP 1: OPEN THE TWO PHOTOS THAT NEED TO BE MERGED TOGETHER

Open the two photos that you're going to be working with. Generally, in one photo you'll have one person (or a group of people) looking good. But there's always that one person that closed their eyes or is looking away from the camera. So you take another photo, and that person looks just fine, but now someone else from the original group (that looked fine before) is looking away. It's great if you realize these things ahead of time, because you can just re-shoot the photo. But if you don't, then it's time to call Photoshop's Auto-Align Layers feature in.

STEP 2: SELECT BOTH LAYERS AND USE THE AUTO-ALIGN LAYERS FEATURE

First, copy-and-paste one of the photos into the other, so they're both in the same document. Then, click on one of the layers in the Layers panel to select it, press-and-hold the Shift key, and click on the other layer to select it, as well. Go to the Edit menu and choose Auto-Align Layers. Leave the Projection set to Auto and click OK. This usually takes a minute as Photoshop examines the details of each layer and uses those key details to line up the top layer with the bottom one. Here, it's done most of the work for me in lining up the photos based on that wall in front of the girls. So, at least they're in relatively the same position and perspective.

STEP 3: CHANGE THE BLEND MODE TO DIFFERENCE AND USE THE MOVE TOOL TO FIX ALIGNMENT

Many times Auto-Align Layers will do the trick right away, and the people will be aligned perfectly. But, the reality is that sometimes you need to do some work yourself. So, let's use an old blend mode trick to align the top layer with the bottom layer. Select the top layer and change the blend mode to Difference. In addition to making your photos look really weird, Difference will show something in black when it's the same on both layers. So my goal here is to get the girl on top to look as dark as possible. Use the Move tool (V) to move the top layer, matching up facial features as much as possible. I also used the V-neck of her shirt as a good reference point to align both layers.

STEP 4: ADD A MASK AND PAINT THE KEY AREAS BACK IN

When you think you're close, go ahead and change the blend mode back to Normal. Then click on the Add Layer Mask icon at the bottom of the Layers panel to add a layer mask. In this example, the little girl on the bottom isn't looking at the camera. But she is on the layer underneath (her sister isn't looking at the camera on that layer, though). So, I selected the Brush tool (B) and painted with black over the girl on the bottom. It hid her face from the top layer and revealed her face from the layer beneath. I also painted in parts of the arm on the right side to make things match up even better. Now, you've got the best parts of each photo in one image.

STEP 5: CROP THE PHOTO

If Auto-Align Layers rotated the photos, too, select the Crop tool (C) from the Toolbox and crop any excess white or transparent areas out of the photo. That's it. Now, you've got the best of both photos, all in one photo.

fx

ENHANCING DEPTH OF FIELD

DEPTH OF FIELD IS ANOTHER GREAT WAY TO BRING MORE FOCUS TO THE SUBJECT IN A PHOTO

If you haven't figured it out yet, this chapter is all about trying to make the subject of a photo look better. That's really one of the main things we're after when enhancing digital photos. We want to make the photo look like it did when we were there. Depth of field is another way to do just that by blurring something. We can do a lot of this work in the camera with our lens and f-stop choices. But, sometimes, the creative idea doesn't strike until the photo hits the computer. This technique will help you fix that.

STEP 1: START OUT WITH A PHOTO THAT HAS A BUSY BACKGROUND THAT IS TOO IN FOCUS

Open a photo that has a busy background in it. Something where the subject is very clear, but the background is too in focus, so it really just distracts from the rest of the image (in this example, the kids are the subject and the parents are the background). Most of the time, you can shoot with a large aperture setting in the camera to try to get this effect, but sometimes it's just not feasible, you don't have the right lens, you don't think about it, or you're simply working on someone else's photo.

©FOTOLIA/MONKEY BUSINESS

STEP 2: DUPLICATE THE BACKGROUND LAYER AND APPLY A GAUSSIAN BLUR FILTER

Duplicate the Background layer by pressing Command-J (PC: Ctrl-J). Click on the Filter menu and choose Blur>Gaussian Blur. The Radius setting really depends on your photo and how much blur you can get away with. Generally, you want to blur it enough so you can still see that something was back there, but you just can't see it in focus. I tend to stick with a setting of 4–5 pixels for low-resolution photos like this one, although since I'm blurring the adults, who are so close behind the kids, I went with a setting of 2 pixels for this photo. For high-res photos, try something around 10–15 pixels. Click OK when you're done.

STEP 3: ADD A LAYER MASK AND PAINT WITH BLACK TO REVEAL THE UNBLURRED KIDS

Click on the Add Layer Mask icon at the bottom of the Layers panel to add a layer mask to the blurred layer. Then, select the Brush tool (B) and choose a soft-edged brush from the Brush Picker. Make sure your Foreground color is set to black, and start painting the unblurred version of the main subject (or subjects, in this case) back in. Depending on what your subject is, you may need to make the brush smaller and zoom in to get the edges. Here, I had to do it to paint the area between the kids back in, as well as the ground near their feet. It may take a minute or two, but it's worth the result and the effect really makes the photo look much stronger.

SELECTIVE SHARPENING

USE LAYERS TO SHARPEN ONLY SPECIFIC PARTS OF THE PHOTO THAT NEED IT MOST

Let's face it, sharpening isn't rocket science. It's actually very simple, so I don't want to complicate it with a bunch of layers and techie terminology. For me, the simplest form of sharpening (and a small amount of it) usually looks the best. However, there are times when some parts of the photo can hold more sharpening than others. That's where this technique comes in. With one layer and a layer mask, we can get a tremendous amount of control in our sharpening.

STEP 1: OPEN A PHOTO THAT NEEDS TO BE SHARPENED

Start off by opening the photo that needs to be sharpened. Here's a photo I took of my niece on Easter Sunday.

MATT KLOSKOWSKI

STEP 2: DUPLICATE THE LAYER AND APPLY THE UNSHARP MASK FILTER

Duplicate the Background layer by pressing Command-J (PC: Ctrl-J), so you have two copies of the image in the Layers panel. Then click the Filter menu and choose Sharpen>Unsharp Mask. This is a low-resolution photo, so I'm going to set the Amount to 150% (that's high for most photos), the Radius to 1.2 pixels, and the Threshold to 0. If it were a higher-resolution photo (150 ppi or higher), I'd use 175%–200% for the Amount. Click OK when you're done to apply the sharpening.

STEP 3: ZOOM IN AND CHECK THE DETAILS

Get the Zoom tool (Z) and click on the photo to zoom in on it (her arms and face are good places to check out). First off, a quick warning: This is actually pretty hard to see in the book, so it's definitely something you'll want to try on your own. In my example, her skin is starting to get a little bit of texture on it, and the edges around her arms have this weird halo around them. That's a dead giveaway of too much sharpening. No problem, we'll take care of that in the next step.

Click on the Add Layer Mask icon at the bottom of the Layers panel to add a layer mask to the top layer (the one we just sharpened). Then press Command-I (PC: Ctrl-I) to invert the white mask and fill it with black instead of white. This hides all of the sharpening effects on the sharpened layer and reveals the original layer beneath.

TIP: I use this one all the time, so read it! Press-and-hold the Option (PC: Alt) key when clicking the Add Layer Mask icon to automatically turn the mask black instead of white.

Get the Brush tool (B) and choose a small, soft-edged brush from the Brush Picker. Make sure your Foreground color is white, and start painting on the mask over the areas in the photo that can use some targeted sharpening. In this example, I've painted on her dress to really bring the detail out. What's great about this technique is that if it doesn't look good, you can just press X to swap your Foreground and Background colors and paint with black to hide the targeted sharpening. Either way, you have a huge amount of control here when it comes to sharpening your photos. At what cost, you ask? Just one extra layer.

BOOSTING SPECIFIC COLORS

FOR THOSE TIMES WHEN ONLY A SPECIFIC COLOR IN A PHOTO NEEDS A BOOST

Often, you'll have a photo where one of the colors just doesn't stand out like it did when you took the photo. One of the benefits of a Hue/Saturation adjustment layer is that you can target specific colors with it, and not the whole photo. Plus, the ability to hide the changes with the layer mask on the adjustment layer can really help create some strong images.

STEP 1: OPEN A PHOTO THAT NEEDS MORE COLOR AND ADD A HUE/SATURATION ADJUSTMENT LAYER

Open a photo where some of the colors just don't have the same punch that the others do. In this example, the yellows and blues look like they could use a little more of a color boost. Go to the Adjustments panel (Window>Adjustments) and click on the Hue/Saturation icon. From the pop-up menu above the Hue slider, choose the color that you want to boost. First, we'll enhance the yellows, so I'm choosing Yellows here.

STEP 2: INCREASE THE SATURATION OF THE DRAB COLORS

Drag the Saturation slider to the right to around +40, and you'll see the yellows become more saturated. This works the same for other colors, too. For example, the sky could use more blue, so choose Blues from the pop-up menu. Now, increase the Saturation setting and you'll see just the blues start to become more vivid.

STEP 3: PAINT ON THE LAYER MASK TO HIDE THE EFFECT EVERYWHERE ELSE

The problem is that anything else that was blue in the photo also became more intense. In this case, the blue building on the right became more saturated, as well, but I kinda liked its less vivid color from before. Since the Hue/Saturation adjustment layer has a mask on it, though, just select the Brush tool (B), choose a soft-edged brush from the Brush Picker, then press X to swap your Foreground and Background colors, making your Foreground color black. Paint with black on the layer mask to hide the effects from the other areas. So now the color boost from the adjustment layer only affects the sky and yellow areas and nothing else.

CREATING SOFT FOCUS

WITH A LAYER AND A FILTER, IT'S EASY TO CREATE THE EFFECT OF A TRADITIONAL PHOTOGRAPHY FILTER

I love to re-create the effect of traditional filters used in photography. The main reason is that I don't have to make the decision about a certain effect when I'm taking the photo. I know I can achieve just as good a result after the fact in Photoshop. That way, I'm not stuck with an effect that I don't want later.

STEP 1: OPEN A PHOTO THAT WOULD BENEFIT FROM A SOFT FOCUS EFFECT

MATT KLOSKOWSKI

Start by opening a photo that would look nice if a soft focus filter had been used when you were taking the photo. Not every photo will work for this. It's probably not good to use a photo of a pair of horses captured neck-and-neck at the finish line. That's not a "soft" photo. Other types of sports photos and really masculine subjects don't work well, either. Portraits of people (couples, or a parent with a child) and early morning photos usually work well, though.

STEP 2: DUPLICATE THE BACKGROUND LAYER AND APPLY THE GAUSSIAN BLUR FILTER

Press Command-J (PC: Ctrl-J) to duplicate the Background layer. Click on the Filter menu and choose Blur>Gaussian Blur. I usually go with a setting of 10 pixels for the Radius, but I'll tell you what to look for when applying the effect: you want to blur the whole photo, but you don't want to blur it to the point where you can't recognize anything in the photo. So, make sure you can still make out the details in the photo before you settle on a Radius setting. Click OK when you're done.

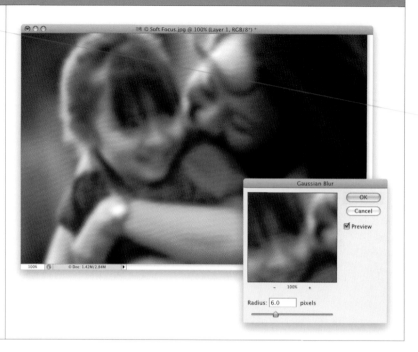

STEP 3: REDUCE THE OPACITY OF THE BLURRED LAYER TO REVEAL THE ORIGINAL LAYER BELOW

After you run the filter, the whole photo will look blurry. The first thing to do is reduce the opacity of the blurred layer. I typically drop it down to around 60%–70%. This reveals more of the original layer that is below.

This part is optional, and really depends on your photo and whether you want to make some areas sharp again. If so, click on the Add Layer Mask icon at the bottom of the Layers panel, then select the Brush tool (B). Press X to change your Foreground color to black, and paint over the main subject in the photo to make it a little sharper than everything else. At this point, you're really done with the soft-focus effect. However, read on if you want to add a nice finishing touch to it.

TIP: After you've painted some of the details back in, try adjusting the Density slider in the Masks panel to fade the mask and bring some softness back if things look too sharp.

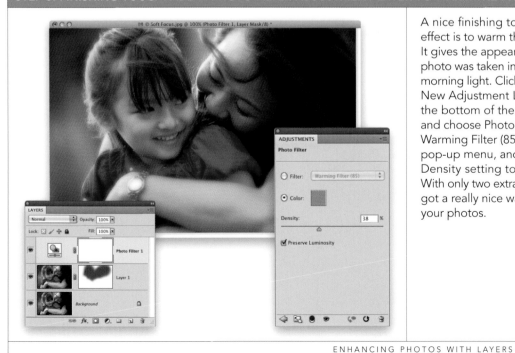

A nice finishing touch for this effect is to warm the photo a bit. It gives the appearance that the photo was taken in that nice, early morning light. Click on the Create New Adjustment Layer icon at the bottom of the Layers panel, and choose Photo Filter. Choose Warming Filter (85) from the Filter pop-up menu, and increase the Density setting to around 40%. With only two extra layers, you've got a really nice way to enhance your photos.

HOW DO I...

QUICKLY DUPLICATE A LAYER?

I know I sound like a broken record, but if there is one keyboard shortcut to get from this whole book, this is it: Press Command-J (PC: Ctrl-J) to quickly duplicate a layer.

MAKE MY BRUSH SOFTER WITHOUT USING THE BRUSH PICKER?

To make your brush harder or softer without going to the Brush Picker, press Shift-[(Left Bracket key) or Shift-] (Right Bracket key).

SET MY FOREGROUND AND BACKGROUND COLORS TO THEIR DEFAULTS (BLACK AND WHITE)?

Just press the letter D to set the Foreground and Background colors to their defaults of black and white. However, if you're working on a layer mask, it's the opposite. Pressing D sets white as the Foreground color and black as the Background color.

SWAP THE FOREGROUND AND BACKGROUND COLORS WITH EACH OTHER?

Press the letter X.

CREATE A NEW LAYER?

To quickly create a new blank layer with no dialogs popping up, press Command-Option-Shift-N (PC: Ctrl-Alt-Shift-N).

QUICKLY CHANGE TO THE OVERLAY BLEND MODE?

Press Option-Shift-O (PC: Alt-Shift-O). If you are using a tool with a blend mode in the Options Bar, this will change the mode there. If you are using a tool without a blend mode in the Options Bar, this will change the current layer's blend mode.

AUTOMATICALLY REAPPLY A FILTER WITH THE SAME SETTINGS?

You can automatically reapply the *last* filter you ran, with the same exact settings, by pressing Command-F (PC: Ctrl-F). You won't even see the dialog.

AUTOMATICALLY REAPPLY A FILTER WITH DIFFERENT SETTINGS?

You can automatically reapply the *last* filter you ran, but this time see the dialog so you can adjust the settings, by pressing Command-Option-F (PC: Ctrl-Alt-F).

CHAPTER SEVEN

RETOUCHING WITH LAYERS

This is one of my favorite topics when it comes to working with layers. It's probably because there is so much you can do with some simple retouching tools and just a couple of layers. Now, as you read this chapter, keep in mind one thing: this isn't meant to be a one-stop shop for all of your retouching needs. Instead, I'd like to show you how to put some of the layer functions that you've seen already to a different use. Plus, there are a few tools in Photoshop for retouching that have some layer-related options that you can use to make your retouching even better.

THE LAYERED TRICK TO REMOVING WRINKLES AND BLEMISHES

THERE ARE A FEW RETOUCHING-SPECIFIC TOOLS IN PHOTOSHOP THAT HAVE A BUILT-IN LAYERS TRICK

When you talk to people in everyday life, you probably don't notice any blemishes or wrinkles that they may have on their faces. This is because you're concentrating (hopefully) on your discussion and interaction with them. However, when you see photos of those same people, you're more likely to notice some small imperfections on their skin. That's where the retouching tools and a couple of layers come in really handy. You can lessen the effect of a person's blemishes and wrinkles, but still be conservative and keep them looking real.

STEP 1: OPEN A PORTRAIT OF SOMEONE THAT HAS A FEW BLEMISHES OR WRINKLES TO REMOVE

Start out by opening a portrait of someone who has a few wrinkles or blemishes that you'd like to remove. If you don't have one you think will work, you can download the image I used here from the website mentioned in the book's introduction.

TIP: If you're going to experiment on a family member or friend, please make sure you're alone first. I've found that no one likes to see their own photo being retouched in Photoshop. I'm just sayin'.

©FOTOLIA/YURI ARCURS

STEP 2: CREATE A NEW BLANK LAYER TO HOLD ALL OF THE RETOUCHING WE'RE ABOUT TO DO

One common theme among many of the layer-related enhancements we've done in this book is to do the work on a separate layer and then drop the layer's opacity to reduce the effect. The same thing goes here. We're going to do all of our retouching on a blank layer, in case we want to bring back some of the original skin below it. So, go ahead and click on the Create a New Layer icon at the bottom of the Layers panel to create a blank layer. You can even name this new layer "Healing" if you want to, because that's what we're going to do. Double-click on the layer name to rename it.

STEP 3: SELECT THE HEALING BRUSH TOOL, AND SET IT TO SAMPLE ALL LAYERS

Next, select the Healing Brush tool from the Toolbox (or just press Shift-J until you have it). Choose a very small, soft-edged brush that is no larger than the size of the area you're about to remove. Now, there is one key setting that makes this layer thing all work. Up in the Options Bar, you'll see a Sample pop-up menu. Make sure you choose All Layers from this menu. If you don't, then none of your work will appear on the blank layer you just created.

TIP: The Healing Brush is just like the regular Brush tool. It has a Diameter setting and a Hardness setting, so use it just like you would any other brush.

STEP 4: OPTION-CLICK (PC: ALT-CLICK) ON A CLEAR PART OF THE SKIN TO SET IT AS A SAMPLE POINT

The Healing Brush works a little differently than it's little brother, the Spot Healing Brush (which we'll cover in another tutorial). With the Spot Healing Brush, you don't have to sample anything. It just melds the spots with the surrounding area. With the Healing Brush, you have to set a sample area to show Photoshop what you want the healed area to look like. This is typically some area of clear skin that is near the area you want to retouch. It doesn't have to be perfectly clean, but better than the wrinkles you want to fix. So, press-and-hold the Option (PC: Alt) key and click on a clear area of skin to serve as the sample point.

STEP 5: PAINT OVER THE WRINKLES WITH THE HEALING BRUSH TO MELD THE SAMPLE AND REAL SKIN

On the Healing layer, paint over the wrinkles or lines just as you would with any brush. Use a brush size that isn't much larger than the actual wrinkle or line itself. Use multiple strokes to continue painting on the wrinkles. Every time you let go of your mouse button, Photoshop will meld the clear, sampled area with the skin you're painting over. You'll see a little crosshair that follows your brush. That is Photoshop's way of telling you where it is sampling from. Most of the time, it does a great job, but if you're not happy with a brush stroke, just press Command-Z (PC: Ctrl-Z) to Undo and try again.

STEP 6: MOVE TO ANOTHER AREA OF THE PHOTO AND CHOOSE ANOTHER PLACE TO SAMPLE FROM

If you've never used the Healing Brush before, you're probably pretty amazed right now. I don't know how it does it, but the behind-the-scenes work that Photoshop is doing is phenomenal.

Next, move to another area of the photo, like the forehead. Since Photoshop remembers where you sampled last, you'll want to Option-click again to sample another area above a forehead wrinkle before you start healing again.

STEP 7: REDUCE THE OPACITY OF THE HEALING BRUSH LAYER

Now, the last thing to do is reduce the opacity of the Healing layer. The removed wrinkles look really fake, but by dropping the layer opacity down to around 40%–50%, you can strike a good balance between real and fake. In the end, you'll have a nice, tastefully retouched portrait.

SMOOTHING AND ENHANCING SKIN

RETOUCHING IS HOT THESE DAYS, AND ONE OF THE FIRST THINGS THAT YOU'LL DO IS SMOOTH THE SKIN

Smoothing skin helps portraits of people of all ages. It's got a few uses: First, you can use it to remove some of the texture that makeup can often leave. Next, you can use it to soften blemishes, acne, freckles, and even the effects of sun damage and wrinkles.

STEP 1: OPEN A PORTRAIT WHERE THE SKIN ON THE FACE NEEDS SOME SMOOTHING

Open a portrait of a person that you'd like to try the skin-smoothing technique on. Read Steps 2 and 3 if you're going to use the same photo that you used in the previous tutorial. I'll show you how to start combining multiple techniques and still manage your layers in your Layers panel. However, if you're starting from scratch, then you can skip to Step 4.

MATT KLOSKOWSKI

If you're reading this step, then I assume you're looking to bring these techniques together. Meaning: you did the first tutorial in this chapter ("The Layered Trick to Removing Wrinkles and Blemishes") and you have an extra layer on top of your Background layer already. Now you want to apply this "Smoothing and Enhancing Skin" technique, but you don't want to flatten your layers. So, at the point of starting this tutorial, your Layers panel should look something like the one here (this is how it looks after finishing the first tutorial).

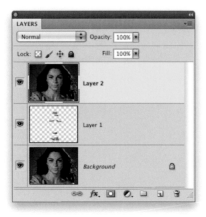

To keep ourselves from having to flatten the image, we can use a keyboard shortcut we've used a few times before in this book that flattens your layers onto a new layer on top of everything else in the Layers panel. Here's what to do: Click on the topmost layer. Then press Command-Option-Shift-E (PC: Ctrl-Alt-Shift-E). It's called Stamp Visible Layers, and it stamps everything that is visible onto a new layer on top of all the others. It lets you flatten to a new layer, but keeps all of your other layers intact. Do this after each technique to give yourself a way out of each one.

STEP 4: DUPLICATE THE BACKGROUND LAYER

If you came here from Step 1, then you should just have a Background layer. If that's the case, press Command-J (PC: Ctrl-J) to duplicate the Background layer, and now there should be two copies of the same layer in the Layers panel.

However, if you came here from Step 3, then you have a flattened layer on top of at least one other layer. Think of this as the "new" Background layer and duplicate it just like you would the normal Background layer.

STEP 5: APPLY THE SURFACE BLUR FILTER TO THE DUPLICATE

Click on the top copy in the Layers panel to make sure it's selected. In order to smooth the skin, we'll have to blur it. A lot of people go straight for the Gaussian Blur filter for this, but I like the Surface Blur filter a lot more. It leaves me with less work to do later (you'll see how in a minute). So, click the Filter menu and choose Blur>Surface Blur. On a low-resolution photo, like the one here, enter 10 pixels for the Radius and set the Threshold to 15. Click OK when you're done.

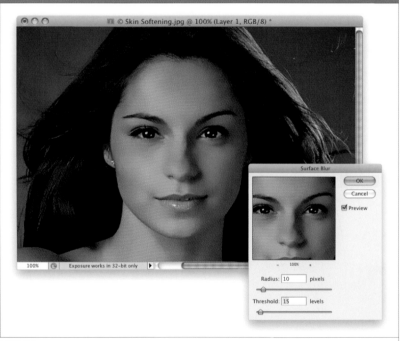

STEP 6: ADD A LAYER MASK TO THE BLURRED LAYER

Now you've blurred the whole photo and the skin should look really smooth. Too smooth, though, right? At this point, it looks very fake. Plus, while the Surface Blur filter does a better job than Gaussian Blur of maintaining the detail areas and just blurring the "surface" or smooth areas, it's not perfect. We still need to bring back those key sharp areas. That's where a layer mask comes in. Click on the Add Layer Mask icon at the bottom of the Layers panel to add a layer mask to the blurred layer.

STEP 7: SELECT THE BRUSH TOOL AND CHOOSE A MEDIUM-SIZED, SOFT-EDGED BRUSH

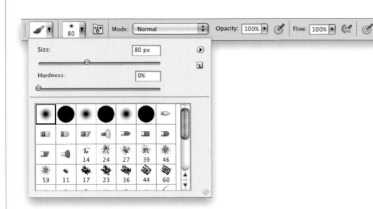

Now select the Brush tool from the Toolbox (or just press the letter B). Click on the brush thumbnail in the Options Bar and select a medium-sized, soft-edged brush from the Brush Picker (something small enough to paint inside the key feature areas, like the eyes and mouth).

STEP 8: PAINT WITH BLACK ON THE LAYER MASK TO REVEAL THE KEY FEATURES FROM BELOW

Press D, then X to set your Foreground color to black. Start painting on the photo on the main features that we want to be sharp. The eyes are the first place to start. Then move on to the nose, the mouth, and any jewelry and hair that should stay sharp, too. Don't forget that you can press the Left and Right Bracket keys to resize your brush quickly.

STEP 9: REDUCE THE OPACITY OF THE BLURRED LAYER TO MAKE THE SKIN LOOK MORE REALISTIC

The last step is optional, but probably recommended depending on how much you blurred the skin. See, some people like that really smooth, porcelain-skin look. It's very common in fashion and glamour photography. However, I'm usually not working for a glamour magazine and I'm not a huge fan of that super-smooth look. So, I reduce the Opacity setting of the blurred layer on top to around 40%–60%. That usually still does a good job of smoothing the skin, but also shows some of the original skin texture from the layer below.

MAKING EYES AND TEETH WHITER

THERE'S ONE ADJUSTMENT THAT TAKES CARE OF TWO VERY COMMON RETOUCHING TASKS

By nature, especially as we age, our eyes tend to get a little darker (and maybe even bloodshot) and our teeth start to take on a yellowish color. It's natural, but there are a few ways that you can lessen those imperfections in photos using Photoshop and make someone look their very best. Even better, there's one adjustment that can take care of both tasks so you can accomplish this with as little as two extra layers.

STEP 1: OPEN A PHOTO WHERE THE EYES OR TEETH NEED WHITENING

If you're combining multiple techniques, merge to a new layer

If not, then just start with the Background layer

©FOTOLIA/MONKEY BUSINESS

All right, start out by opening a photo where the eyes or teeth need whitening. Or both, if you have one. This photo can actually use a little of both adjustments, but we'll work on one area at a time. If you've already done some retouching like we did in the previous two tutorials in this chapter, then you already have some layers. If you want to save those layers, then use the trick mentioned in Step 3 of the previous technique—just press Command-Option-Shift-E (PC: Ctrl-Alt-Shift-E) to merge everything into one new layer on top of the original layers. That'll be your New Background layer (seen here). If not, then just start out with the Background layer.

STEP 2: ADD A HUE/SATURATION ADJUSTMENT LAYER, CHOOSE REDS, AND REDUCE THE SATURATION

First, let's work on the eyes. Go to the Adjustments panel and add a Hue/Saturation adjustment layer. One of the common problems with eyes is that they tend to have some red in them. So, choose Reds from the pop-up menu near the top and reduce the Saturation setting. I know, things get pretty scary-looking at this point, but don't worry. We'll fix it in a minute.

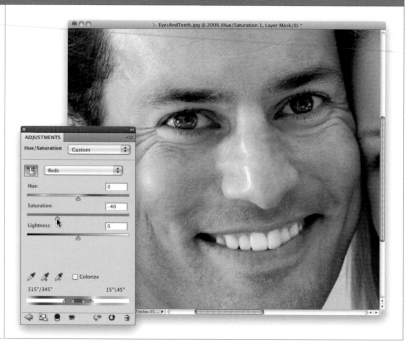

STEP 3: SWITCH BACK TO MASTER AND INCREASE THE LIGHTNESS SETTING

Next, switch back to the Master setting in the pop-up menu and increase the Lightness setting to 20 to lighten the whole photo.

STEP 4: FILL THE MASK WITH BLACK. USE THE BRUSH TOOL TO PAINT WITH WHITE ON THE EYES

Since the whole photo looks really bad and we just want to fix a small area, let's fill the adjustment layer mask with black. Just press Command-I (PC: Ctrl-I) to invert the white and make it black. That hides the Hue/Saturation adjustment. Now, use the Zoom tool (Z) to zoom in on the eyes. Press D to set your Foreground to white, select the Brush tool (B) and paint with white over the whites of his eyes. You'll probably have to use a small brush and take your time, but it should only take a minute or so. When you're done, drop the adjustment layer's opacity to around 80% to make the whiter eyes more believable.

STEP 5: MOVE ON TO THE TEETH FOR WHITENING. MAKE A SELECTION OF THE TEETH FIRST

Now, let's move on to the teeth. This time, let's make a selection first. Select the teeth with your favorite selection tool. I used the Quick Selection tool (W) for this photo and just clicked on the teeth until they were all selected. Don't worry if you get a little of the gums in there, we'll fix that later. Just make sure you get all the teeth.

STEP 6: ADD ANOTHER HUE/SATURATION ADJUSTMENT FOR THE TEETH. THIS TIME, CHOOSE YELLOWS

Add another Hue/Saturation adjustment layer by clicking on the Create New Adjustment Layer icon at the bottom of the Layers panel and choosing Hue/Saturation. This time, choose Yellows from the pop-up menu near the top of the Adjustments panel.

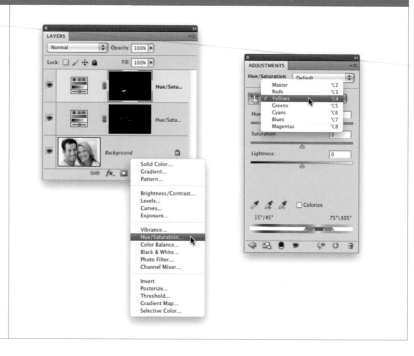

STEP 7: DRAG THE SATURATION TO THE LEFT. GO BACK TO MASTER AND INCREASE LIGHTNESS

Bring the Saturation setting all the way to the left. Then, just like before, switch the pop-up menu back to Master, and increase the Lightness setting—just a little—to around 5. Notice how the adjustment is just being restricted to the area we selected back in Step 5. You'll also see that, even though we have two Hue/Saturation adjustment layers on top of each other, the changes aren't being applied to the whole photo. That's because each layer mask allows each adjustment layer to show only a small part of its adjustment (eyes and teeth).

STEP 8: USE THE BRUSH TOOL TO TWEAK THE LAYER MASK IN CASE THE SELECTION WASN'T PERFECT

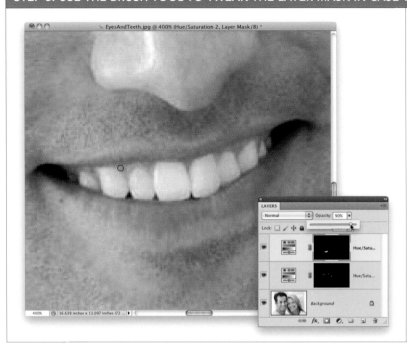

Once again, select the Brush tool (B) and use the Zoom tool (Z) to zoom in on the teeth. Make sure your Foreground color is white, and paint on any areas that may not have gotten selected the first time. Or, press X to switch your Foreground and Background colors, and paint with black to hide the changes from areas that your selection may have spilled over into accidentally. Drop the opacity of the Hue/Saturation adjustment layer if the teeth start to look too white. Now you have whitened the eyes and the teeth with just two layers.

BEFORE AND AFTER

Before

After

REMOVING DISTRACTIONS

RETOUCHING ISN'T RESTRICTED TO PEOPLE. ANY PHOTO WITH A DISTRACTION IN IT IS FAIR GAME

Now we're going to take a look at a few different ways to remove distractions. In this tutorial, we'll use the Clone Stamp tool. It's a lot like the Healing Brush that we used earlier in this chapter, but you'll see it's also very different. Then, we'll take a look at some of the new Content-Aware features in Photoshop CS5, and you'll see that each of the tools we talk about has a special layers-related function, too.

STEP 1: OPEN A PHOTO WITH SOME DISTRACTIONS THAT NEED TO BE REMOVED

Open a photo with some distractions or unwanted areas in it. We're going to start simple with a photo I took in Dubai. It's a gorgeous mosque that is just about flawless in every way. However, when I took the photo there was a bird flying through, and you'll also see there's a small security camera on the wall (near the center of the image) that's kind of distracting. We'll use the Clone Stamp tool to remove them, because it'll do a better job removing these things than the Healing Brush would do (the Healing Brush leaves a weird-looking texture on the wall).

MATT KLOSKOWSKI

STEP 2: CREATE A NEW LAYER TO HOLD THE RETOUCHING WORK WE'RE ABOUT TO DO

Just like we did when retouching the portraits, click on the Create a New Layer icon at the bottom of the Layers panel to create a new blank layer to hold our retouching work.

STEP 3: GET THE CLONE STAMP TOOL. MAKE SURE SAMPLE ALL LAYERS IS SELECTED

Select the Clone Stamp tool from the Toolbox, or press the letter S to get it. The Clone Stamp tool is a lot like the Healing Brush tool. It's got the same Sample pop-up menu in the Options Bar. Make sure you choose All Layers from this pop-up menu so we can do our work on the blank layer. Otherwise, when we sample a point with the Clone Stamp tool, it'll just sample from the transparent layer (which has nothing on it).

STEP 4: OPTION-CLICK (PC: ALT-CLICK) ON A CLEAN AREA TO SET IT AS A SAMPLE POINT

I mentioned that the Clone Stamp tool is a lot like the Healing Brush. So much so that you've got to set a sample point with it just like we did in the Healing Brush tutorial. You've got to be a little more careful when setting the sample point with the Clone Stamp tool, though. It doesn't meld areas together like the Healing Brush; it copies them exactly. That's the main difference. So you'll want to sample an area that's close to what you're going to be cloning. Option-click (PC: Alt-click) on the wall directly next to where you're cloning to set it as the clone sample point (it'll help if you sample a texture or pattern that matches, too). Use the Zoom tool (Z) to zoom in, if necessary.

STEP 5: USE THE CLONE OVERLAY TO MAKE SURE YOUR CLONING MATCHES

Back in Photoshop CS4, Adobe added a clone overlay feature that puts an overlay (in other words, a preview) of what you just sampled into your brush (because the Clone Stamp tool is really just a brush that clones). I gotta say, this tiny feature makes cloning so much easier. Since I sampled a pattern that looks the same as what I want to paint over, I can use that overlay to preview my cloning and make that pattern fit perfectly. So, before you click to paint, make sure everything is lined up first when you move your brush over the area you want to remove.

STEP 6: START PAINTING TO REMOVE THE DISTRACTION

Click-and-drag to paint (clone) your source area over the distraction (in this case, the bird). Just like the Healing Brush, you'll see that little crosshair following your cursor, showing you where Photoshop is sampling from.

STEP 7: OPTION-CLICK AGAIN IN ANOTHER PART OF THE PHOTO TO SET ANOTHER SAMPLE POINT

Since the Clone Stamp tool is a little more finicky than the Healing Brush, we're going to set another sample point to remove the camera. Option-click on another point right next to the camera. Once you've sampled, remember that your cursor now shows you a preview of the clone source area, so move that into place before you start painting. Then, click-and-drag with the Clone Stamp tool to clone the camera away.

CONTENT-AWARE FILL: IT'S CLONING AND HEALING COMBINED!

TAKE THE BEST OF THE CLONE STAMP TOOL AND THE BEST OF THE HEALING BRUSH AND PUT THEM TOGETHER

At this point in the chapter, you've seen where the Healing Brush comes in handy. It's great for removing distractions and retouching photos in a way that blends the problem area with the surrounding area. But it's not good for details. You've also seen the Clone Stamp tool. If you need to be precise and copy an area from one portion of a photo to another, pixel-for-pixel, the Clone Stamp tool is the way to go. Well, there's one tool that we've left out—it's called the Spot Healing Brush, but honestly, the name doesn't do it justice. It lets you clone and heal at the same time and it's got a new feature in CS5 called Content-Aware, and let me tell ya, you've got to see it to believe it.

STEP 1: OPEN A PHOTO WITH SOME AREAS THAT NEED TO BE REMOVED

In the photo that we're working with here, there are a few things I'd like to remove. First, there are a few lens flare spots in the sky. Then, there's that shadow being cast of the person that was holding the flash. I was able to crop them out of the photo in-camera, but their shadow is still there. Could I remove these areas with a careful combination of the Clone Stamp tool and the Healing Brush? Yup. But what you're about to see here makes it much easier.

STEP 2: ADD A NEW LAYER TO HOLD THE RETOUCHING WE'RE ABOUT TO DO

Just like everything else we've done in this chapter, your retouching in this project is all going to be done on its own layer. This comes in really handy because you can go back to this layer and erase, enhance, or change one specific part of your retouching work without affecting the rest of it. If you did the work all on the photo layer, then you'd have to undo all of your work just to get back to a point earlier. So, click on the Create a New Layer icon at the bottom of the Layers panel to add a new layer for our retouching.

STEP 3: SELECT THE SPOT HEALING BRUSH AND MAKE SURE THE CONTENT-AWARE OPTION IS TURNED ON

All right, remember how I mentioned in the intro that the Spot Healing Brush lets you clone and heal at the same time? It's not a new tool, but it's got a brand new option that might as well make it a new tool. I know the name doesn't sound like it does anything cooler or better, but it does. In fact, I can honestly say it's one of the most powerful retouching tools in Photoshop. So, select it from the Toolbox (or press J) and, in the Options Bar, choose a small, soft-edged brush, make sure the Content-Aware radio button is selected, and turn on the Sample All Layers checkbox.

STEP 4: START SIMPLE. PAINT ON THE LENS FLARE SPOTS IN THE SKY

Let's start off simple here. The Spot Healing Brush works a little differently than the Healing Brush and Clone Stamp tools do. Remember how we had to press-and-hold the Option (PC: Alt) key to sample an area first? Well, you don't have to do that with the Spot Healing Brush. It automatically looks at what's around the area you paint and makes a choice for you. Try it. Just paint on the small lens flare and sensor dust spots in the sky (you may need to zoom in to see them better) and you'll see them disappear pretty fast. No sweat, right? The Spot Healing Brush lives up to its name and removes spots pretty quickly.

STEP 5: REMOVE THE SHADOW ON THE GROUND NEXT

Next, paint one continuous stroke over the shadow on the ground and watch what happens. First off, what you see on your photo may be different from what you see here. The Content-Aware option can be a little random (not much, though), so you might not get exactly the same results. But what you should see is that Photoshop removed most of the shadow. It kinda blended the area, but it kinda cloned parts around it, too. That's why I said it's the perfect mix of both tools. If your results are like mine, though, it didn't remove everything. In fact, it may have even added a few weird areas. That's normal and I picked this example, because I think it's real. Content-Aware, along with the Spot Healing brush, got 90% of the job done.

STEP 6: SWITCH TO THE CLONE STAMP TOOL TO CLEAN THINGS UP

Like I said, in the previous step, we're 90% of the way there. This would have taken a lot longer if we just used the Clone Stamp tool, so the Spot Healing Brush definitely helped out. However, we're going to switch to the Clone Stamp tool (S) to clean the shadow area up. Make sure All Layers is selected in the Sample pop-up menu in the Options Bar, then Option-click on an area below the old shadow to sample a clean spot. Now paint over the stuff that the Spot Healing Brush created back in Step 5. That should do it for the shadow. Don't forget, all of this is on a separate layer, so you can always get back to your original or adjust the layer if you need to blend it with the original.

BEFORE AND AFTER

Before

After

HOW DO I...

DO MY RETOUCHING ON A BLANK LAYER?

To retouch on a blank layer, make sure you select the Sample All Layers option in the Options Bar for the tool you're using (this works for the Spot Healing Brush, the Healing Brush, and the Clone Stamp tool). Then, create a blank layer and make sure it's selected when you're retouching.

LESSEN THE EFFECT OF ANY RETOUCHING I'VE DONE ON A LAYER?

The best way to lessen any retouching effect is to do the retouching on a separate blank layer and then reduce the opacity of that layer to bring in the original texture, pattern, or object from the layer below.

FLATTEN MY LAYERS WITHOUT ACTUALLY FLATTENING THEM?

This is one of my favorite little tricks. Flattening without flattening is very useful. Say you want to work on a flattened layer of the work you've done thus far, but you don't want to actually flatten all of the layers in your Layers panel. Click on the top layer in your Layers panel. Then, press Command-Option-Shift-E (PC: Ctrl-Alt-Shift-E). This creates a new layer and stamps all of the layers under it onto that new layer. But, it leaves all the layers intact so they're not actually flattened.

QUICKLY SWITCH TO YELLOWS IN THE HUE/SATURATION OPTIONS IN THE ADJUSTMENTS PANEL?

Just press Option-4 (PC: Alt-4). In fact, all of the colors in the Hue/Saturation options in the Adjustments panel have a shortcut key. They range from Option-2 (PC: Alt-2) through Option-8 (PC: Alt-8) (just check the pop-up menu for the rest).

CHAPTER EIGHT

LAYER STYLES

Photoshop has a bunch of layer effects (known as layer styles), such as shadows, glows, bevels, and strokes, that can be instantly applied to any layer. That, in and of itself, is a great time saver. However, layer styles take it a step further in two ways: 1) You can always edit them. They're live effects, so you can add a 4-pixel white stroke around a layer and later decide to go back and make it a 2-pixel stroke instead. 2) You can save them. This lets you make a style that you really like, save it, and open another photo and apply that same style to it with just a click. There are literally thousands of combinations with layer styles, so roll your sleeves up and get ready to be wowed if you've never seen them in action before.

fx

LAYER STYLE BASICS

YOU CAN CREATE SOME REALLY EYE-CATCHING DESIGNS WITH A FEW SIMPLE LAYER STYLES

The beauty of layer styles is their simplicity. They're easy to add, easy to save, and easy to change (if you ever need to). Plus, they're built right into Photoshop. Effects that used to be a total pain in the neck to add to an image are now just a click away. Drop shadows, strokes, glows, bevels…the whole nine yards. I'm tellin' ya, if you haven't messed around with layer styles for design purposes yet, then you owe it to yourself to read this tutorial, and the rest of the chapter.

STEP 1: OPEN A PHOTO TO APPLY AN EFFECT TO

Open a photo to apply a layer style design effect to. The example we're going to create here works great on people in motion and sports photos. If you want to follow along using this same image, go to the book's download website listed in the introduction.

©FOTOLIA/ALEKSEY IPATOV

STEP 2: SELECT THE SUBJECT FROM THE BACKGROUND AND PUT HIM ON HIS OWN LAYER

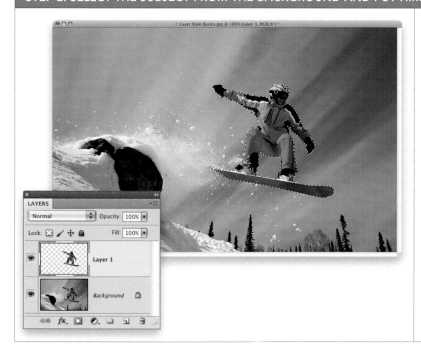

First things first. You have to select your main subject off of the photo's background. Here, I've used the Quick Selection tool (W) to put a selection around the snowboarder (don't forget, back in Chapter 4 we looked at the Refine Edge dialog, which can help refine your selection, as well). After you make the selection, press Command-J (PC: Ctrl-J) to put the selection up onto its own layer.

STEP 3: MAKE A RECTANGULAR SELECTION OF THE BACKGROUND AREA YOU WANT TO INCLUDE

Click on the Background layer to select it again. Then use the Rectangular Marquee tool (M) to make a rectangular selection around the part of the photo you want to keep. Make sure the selection includes part of the snowboader. That way, he'll appear to be jumping out of the photo later. Once again, press Command-J to put this rectangular selection up onto its own layer.

STEP 4: CLICK ON THE ADD A LAYER STYLE ICON AT THE BOTTOM OF THE LAYERS PANEL

Make sure the rectangular photo layer that you just made in the previous step is still selected. We're going to put a stroke around the photo, but in a different way than we've done it in this book so far. At the bottom of the Layers panel, you'll see the fx icon. This is the Add a Layer Style icon. Click on it to see the pop-up menu of layer styles that you can add.

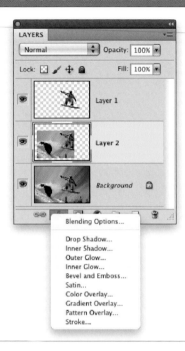

STEP 5: ADD A STROKE LAYER STYLE

Choose Stroke from the pop-up menu to open the Layer Style dialog. You'll see that Stroke is already chosen on the left, and the Stroke settings are open. Change the Size to 15 pixels. Set the Position to Inside. Finally, next to Color at the bottom, click on the color swatch and change the color to white.

TIP: Setting the Position to Inside makes the stroke edges crisp instead of rounded.

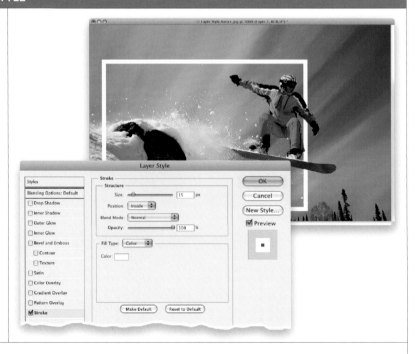

STEP 6: ADD A DROP SHADOW LAYER STYLE TO LIFT THE SELECTION OFF THE BACKGROUND

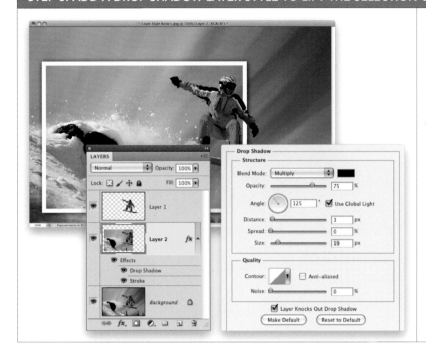

Click on Drop Shadow on the left of the Layer Style dialog to add a Drop Shadow layer style to the layer, too. Here's a tip, though: make sure you don't just turn on the checkbox, but actually click on the words "Drop Shadow" to see the right settings. Change the Angle setting to 125, the Distance to 3, and the size to 19 pixels. Click OK to close the dialog. You'll be able to see the styles in the Layers panel.

STEP 7: ADD A DROP SHADOW LAYER STYLE TO THE LAYER WITH THE SUBJECT ON IT

Now let's add a layer style to the layer with the snowboarder. Instead of adding a new shadow, we can copy an existing one from another layer. Just press-and-hold the Option (PC: Alt) key and click-and-drag the Drop Shadow layer style from the photo layer we just added it to, to the layer with the snowboarder selection. Release your mouse button over the layer with the snowboarder on it, and you'll see the Drop Shadow layer style gets copied to it. However, this shadow not only falls on the outside of the photo but on the inside, as well. We'll take care of that in Step 10.

To make things easier to see and more pleasing overall, click on the Background layer and fill it with white. To do this, press D to set your Background color to white, then press Command-Delete (PC: Ctrl-Backspace) to fill the layer with your Background color. This gives a nice backdrop for the "breaking out of the photo" effect we're creating.

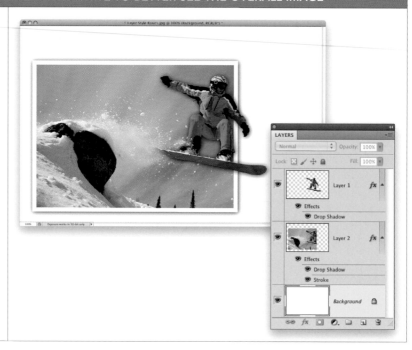

If you want to see what your image looks like without a specific layer style applied to it, click on the little Eye icon next to the Drop Shadow layer style in the Layers panel to hide just that layer style. You'll still see the Stroke layer style, though, but the drop shadow is temporarily hidden. Just click where the Eye icon was to turn it back on.

TIP: If you want to delete the drop shadow altogether, just click on the Drop Shadow layer style in the Layers panel and drag it onto the Trash icon at the bottom of the panel.

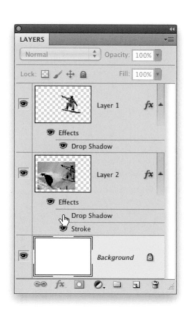

STEP 10: TURN THE DROP SHADOW LAYER STYLE INTO A REGULAR LAYER

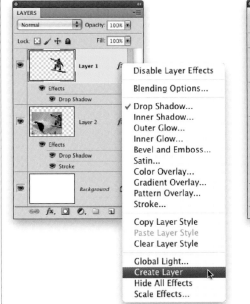

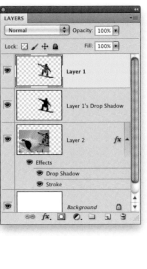

One problem that is left with this image is that the shadow behind the snowboarder is unrealistic. See, it should indeed fall on the area outside the rectangular photo. That's what gives the effect of him "breaking out" of the photo. However, there shouldn't be a shadow on top of the photo itself. To fix this, we need to turn the effects of the layer style into a regular layer. Right-click on the *fx* icon on the right side of the layer. From the pop-up menu, choose Create Layer. This renders the layer style to its own layer below the snowboarder. It's not an editable layer style anymore, but we can go in and erase from it now.

STEP 11: ERASE AWAY THE UNWANTED AREAS FROM THE DROP SHADOW

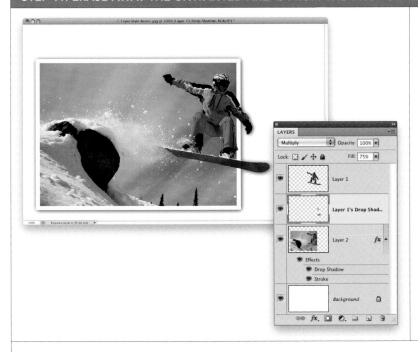

Make sure you have the drop shadow layer selected, then select the Eraser tool (E) and erase away the areas where the shadow appears over the rectangular photo. However, leave the drop shadow wherever it extends past the white stroke edge to give the appearance that the snowboarder is indeed breaking out of the photo.

STEP 12: CENTER THE PHOTO AND SNOWBOARDER

If you want to center your photo with the snowboarder breaking out of it on the white background, just click on the first layer above the Background layer, then Command-click (PC: Ctrl-click) on each layer above that one to select them all. Now, use the Move tool (V) to click on the photo and move it into the center of your document.

CREATING A WATERMARK

LAYER STYLES ACTUALLY HAVE TWO OPACITY SETTINGS THAT CAN BE USED FOR
DIFFERENT EFFECTS

Throughout this book, we've duplicated a layer many times, applied an effect to the duplicate, and then reduced the opacity of the layer. All along we've been reducing the actual Opacity setting, but you may have seen a Fill (opacity) setting in the Layers panel, as well. Here's where you'll learn what the difference is.

STEP 1: OPEN AN IMAGE TO WATERMARK. ADD YOUR COPYRIGHT

Open any image that you want to protect or watermark. This technique is really useful for images you want to place on the Web, but don't want people to steal or use without paying you. The first thing you need to do is add the shape that you want to use as the watermark. It could be your company logo, your initials, or just a copyright symbol (you can make one with the Custom Shape tool). Here, I've used a graphic with my name on it that I copied-and-pasted onto my photo.

STEP 2: ADD A BEVEL AND EMBOSS LAYER STYLE TO YOUR COPYRIGHT OR LOGO LAYER

Double-click on your copyright or logo layer to open the Layer Style dialog. Click on Bevel and Emboss on the left side of the dialog to open those settings. Change the Depth setting to around 80%, and the Size to 1. Click OK to close the dialog.

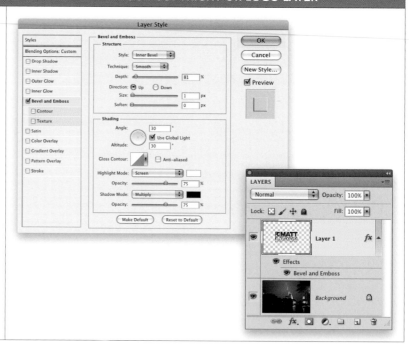

STEP 3: REDUCE THE FILL OPACITY

In order for this to work as a watermark, you need to see through the black area. If you just decrease the layer's Opacity setting, you'll definitely make the black part of the shape or logo see-through, but you'll also hide the Bevel and Emboss layer style, which is key to the watermark effect. Instead, near the top of the Layers panel, reduce the Fill setting to 0%. Doing this hides the pixels that are on the layer (in this case, my black name graphic), but leaves any layer style effects. Here, that means we see the Bevel and Emboss layer style, which is what gives the appearance of a watermark.

CREATING REUSABLE PHOTO EFFECTS

LAYER STYLES ARE GREAT FOR CREATING EYE-CATCHING AND REUSABLE PHOTO EFFECTS

Many Photoshop users out there typically think of layer styles as a "design" effect. That is, as something that designers would use more than photographers. Honestly, that's partly true, but there are some great photographic examples of layer styles, too. In fact, they really come in handy when it comes to creating reusable photographic effects, because you create them once, save them, and then apply them to other photos with just one click. Let's take a look.

STEP 1: OPEN A PHOTO AND TURN THE BACKGROUND LAYER INTO A REGULAR LAYER

MATT KLOSKOWSKI

Start out by opening the photo that you're going to apply the layer style effect to. Here, we're going to apply a classic tint. One little nuance about layer styles is that you can't apply them to a Background layer. So, double-click on the Background layer, and click OK in the New Layer dialog to turn it into a regular layer.

STEP 2: ADD A COLOR OVERLAY LAYER STYLE AND CHANGE THE COLOR TO BROWN

Double-click on the layer to open the Layer Style dialog. Click on Color Overlay on the left side. This will turn your whole photo to an ugly red (the default tint). First, click on the color swatch to the right of the Blend Mode pop-up menu, and change it to the color you want to tint your photo. I'm choosing an orangey/brown here (R: 111, G: 91, B: 51).

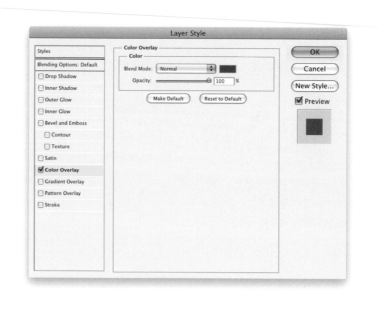

STEP 3: CHANGE THE BLEND MODE IN THE COLOR OVERLAY STYLE TO COLOR

At this point, you'll still only be able to see a solid color on your photo. To see through the color, change the Blend Mode pop-up menu to Color. This uses the color you just chose to tint the overall photo. If it's too much color tint, then drop the Opacity setting to 60%–70%.

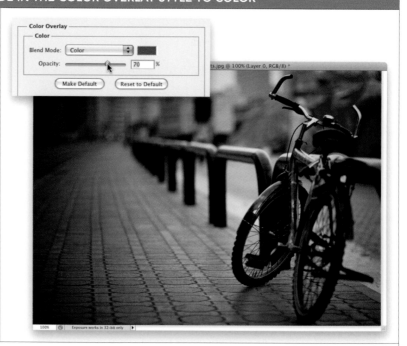

STEP 4: ADD AN INNER GLOW. CHANGE THE COLOR TO BLACK AND BLEND MODE TO MULTIPLY

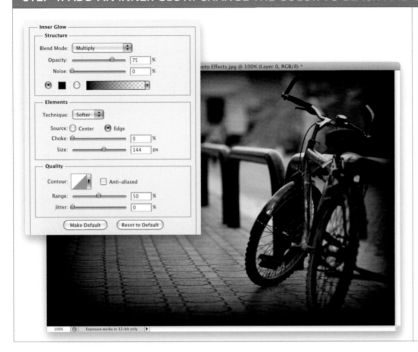

To bring this effect home, click on Inner Glow on the left to show those settings. Inner Glow is set to put a yellowish glow inside your photo. But we're going to use it for an edge-darkening effect. First, click on the color swatch and change the color to black. Then, change the Blend Mode pop-up menu to Multiply. Finally, increase the Size setting to something large (like 140 px, or maybe higher if you have a high-res photo). If it's too much and too dark, drop the Opacity setting down to 30%–40%. Don't click OK yet, though.

STEP 5: SAVE THE LAYER STYLE AS A REUSABLE PRESET

Take a look over at the right side of the dialog. See the New Style button? Click on that button to open the New Style dialog. Give your style a descriptive name and click OK to save it. Now you've saved this style so you can use it again later. Go ahead and click OK to close the Layer Style dialog.

STEP 6: OPEN ANOTHER PHOTO THAT YOU'D LIKE TO APPLY THE SAME EFFECT TO

You can save-and-close the first photo now. You're done with that one. Go ahead and open another photo that you'd like to apply the same effect to.

MATT KLOSKOWSKI

STEP 7: OPEN THE STYLES PANEL. FIND THE STYLE YOU JUST CREATED

Now that you've opened another photo to apply the style to, you've got to find the style, right? Just click the Window menu and choose Styles. This opens the Styles panel. Here is where all your preset layer styles live. If you scroll to the very bottom, you'll see the Classic Tint style we just created.

TIP: If you click the arrow at the top right of the Styles panel to open the panel's flyout menu, you'll see there are lots of preset styles that Photoshop ships with, and they're all already on your computer. Give 'em a try.

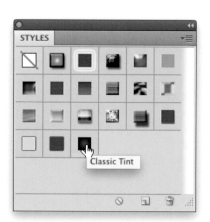

Now just click on the Classic Tint style icon in the Styles panel to apply it to the new photo. Don't forget that it won't work until you've converted the Background layer to a regular layer.

You're pretty much done, but let's say you want to change some aspect of the style, like the color you chose in Color Overlay. Just double-click on the Color Overlay layer style's name in the Layers panel to open the Layer Style dialog to those settings, and change the color to whatever you like. That's the cool thing about layer styles. They're live effects, meaning you can always go back and change them at any point.

SOME MORE LAYER STYLE IDEAS

HERE ARE A FEW MORE IDEAS WHEN IT COMES TO USING LAYER STYLES

I mentioned earlier that there were literally thousands of possibilities when it comes to what you can do with layer styles. There are, and I can't list them all, but here are a few of my favorites:

IDEA 1: GLOWING LIGHT STREAKS

I picked this style up from the National Association of Photoshop Professionals' Photoshop special effects wizard, Corey Barker. Just grab your Brush tool and choose any one of the jagged-texture-looking brushes from the Brush Picker. Paint some strokes onto your image and add both Inner Glow and Outer Glow layer styles to make them look like neon glowing light streaks.

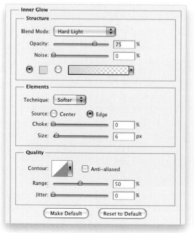

Inner Glow

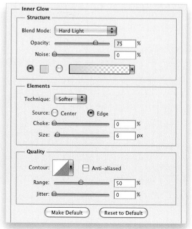

Outer Glow

Final Image

IDEA 2: ROCK TEXTURE

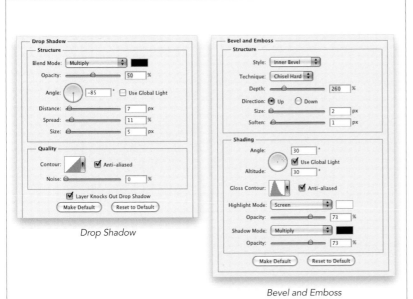

Drop Shadow

Bevel and Emboss

You can also add a rock-like texture to your images. It works great on text, but you can use it on just about any shape you'd like. It also looks really cool when you place it on top of something that has an old, worn, or rusty feel to it. *Note:* For the Pattern Overlay layer style, you'll have to add the Rock Patterns to your Pattern Picker.

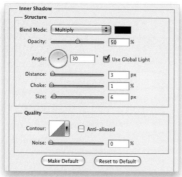

Gradient Overlay

Inner Shadow

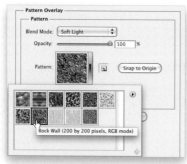

Pattern Overlay

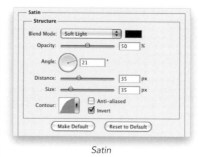

Satin

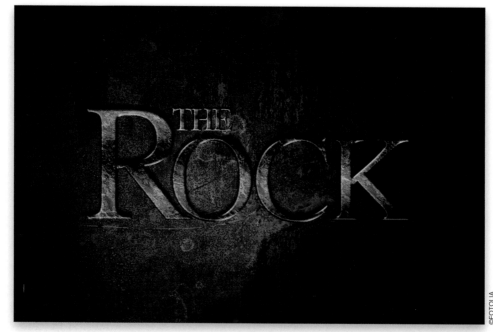

Final Image

IDEA 3: BURNT/CARVED-IN-WOOD EFFECT

Layer styles are also great for making an object look like it's carved into the surface that it's on. This style not only does that, but adds a burned-in effect to it, as well. The key is to put this over a texture that looks like it could have something carved into it.

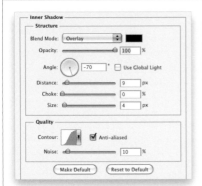

Inner Shadow

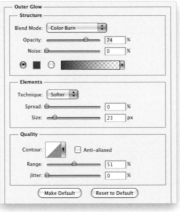

Outer Glow

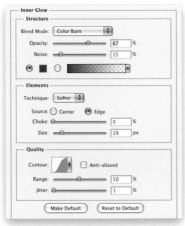

Inner Glow

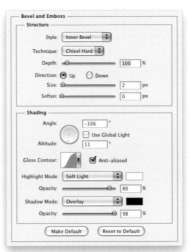

Bevel and Emboss

Gradient Overlay

Final Image

Layer styles are great for other special effects, too. If you ever want to give your text a plastic or watery look, then give this one a try. For the underwater look, I just warped the text (by clicking the Create Warped Text icon in the Options Bar after typing my text).

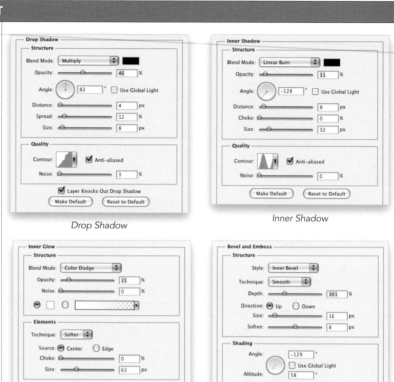

Drop Shadow

Inner Shadow

Inner Glow

Bevel and Emboss

Final Image

HOW DO I...

ADD A LAYER STYLE TO A LAYER?

Double-click on the layer thumbnail or an open area on the layer, and that will open the Layer Style dialog.

QUICKLY DUPLICATE A LAYER STYLE?

Press-and-hold the Option (PC: Alt) key and click-and-drag the layer style you want to duplicate to the layer you want to add it to.

TURN OFF JUST ONE LAYER STYLE OUT OF SEVERAL THAT I'VE APPLIED TO A LAYER?

Say you've applied Drop Shadow, Bevel and Emboss, and Stroke layer styles to a layer. To turn off just the drop shadow, click on the Eye icon next to it in the Layers panel. It'll still be there, but it won't be visible anymore.

DELETE A LAYER STYLE?

Drag the small *fx* icon in the Layers panel to the Trash icon at the bottom. Or, you can Right-click on it and choose Clear Style.

SAVE A LAYER STYLE

In the Layer Style dialog, click on the New Style button in the top right. Give your style a descriptive name and click OK.

SEE MY SAVED LAYER STYLES?

Your saved layer styles live in the Styles panel. Click the Window menu and choose Styles to see them.

APPLY A SAVED LAYER STYLE?

Open the Styles panel, then select the layer you want to apply the style to in the Layers panel, and click on the style in the Styles panel to apply it.

TURN ANY APPLIED LAYER STYLES INTO A REGULAR LAYER?

Layer styles are always editable, even after you've applied them. However, to turn them into regular layers that you can paint and erase on, just Right-click on the layer style icon in the Layers panel and choose Create Layer(s).

MAKE THE LIGHTING ANGLE ON ONE LAYER STYLE DIFFERENT FROM THE ANGLE ON ANOTHER?

Let's say you've added three Drop Shadow layer styles to three different layers. By default, the Angle setting will be the same for all three. If you change it for one layer, it will change for all three. To get around this, in the Layer Style dialog, turn off the Use Global Light checkbox for the layer style you're working on. That will let you change its Angle independently.

CHAPTER NINE

SMART LAYERS

In previous versions of Photoshop (CS3 and CS4), Adobe started doing some really neat things with layers. They're making them indestructible. This means that you can now do things to layers like transforming, resizing, warping, and replacing—nondestructively. This always gives you an out and always gives you a way back, in case something in your image changes as time goes on. In Photoshop CS5, you can even apply a filter to a layer and then go back to change the filter settings at any time. So, the moral of this story is that Photoshop's layers keep getting smarter and smarter. Turn the page and read this chapter to find out how.

fx

FIVE REASONS WHY SMART OBJECTS ROCK!

SMART OBJECTS FLAT OUT ROCK! HERE ARE FIVE REASONS WHY

If you're the type who likes to learn hands-on, then feel free to skip this tutorial and jump to the next one. It's a real-world project all about Smart Objects, and showcases all of the great features that they have. However, if you just want a quick lesson on what Smart Objects are and why you'd want to use them, then read this tutorial first.

STEP 1: CREATING A SMART OBJECT

Before you jump into the reasons why Smart Objects rock, you've got to know what they are and how to create them. First, a Smart Object layer is a special kind of layer that is basically indestructible. Everything you do to it is non-destructive and reversible. You'll see how in a minute. To create a Smart Object layer, click the File menu and choose Open as Smart Object. Then choose an image or photo to open.

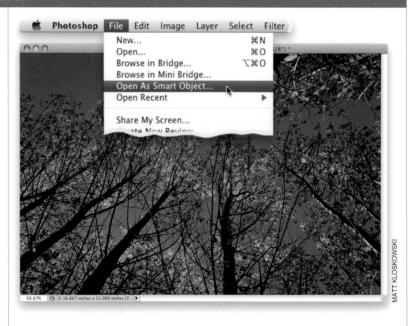

MATT KLOSKOWSKI

STEP 2: LOOK AT THE LAYERS PANEL. THE LAYER LOOKS A LITTLE DIFFERENT THAN NORMAL

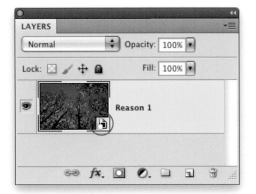

Now look over in the Layers panel. You'll see a layer there just like you'd normally expect. However, look a little closer at it and you'll notice an icon (circled here in red) in the bottom-right corner of the layer thumbnail. That icon means the layer is a Smart Object layer. Everything else should still look the same. There…you've created your first Smart Object layer. Now, on to the five reasons why Smart Objects rock!

REASON 1: SMART OBJECTS = SMART FILTERS

Every time we've run a filter in this book, it's been a permanent change to the layer. The only way to go back and change the settings of that filter is to undo all of your changes. However, there's a nifty little feature in Photoshop called Smart Filters. It lets you run a filter on a layer (through the Filter menu, just like you normally would), but then you can go back and change it at any time. However, Smart Filters can only be added to Smart Object layers. Here, I used a new filter called OilPaint to get this way cool effect (but any filter will work). It's an awesome new filter available through http://labs.adobe .com under "Pixel Bender." Download it and give it a try—you'll get addicted.

REASON 2A: SMART OBJECTS ARE RESIZABLE

Smart Objects are also infinitely resizable. This means that you can open an image as a Smart Object (like maybe a logo). Then make it smaller. Then make it larger again. Then make it smaller and larger again, and never lose any image quality. If you tried this on a non–Smart Object layer you'd probably get something that looked like the last image you see here.

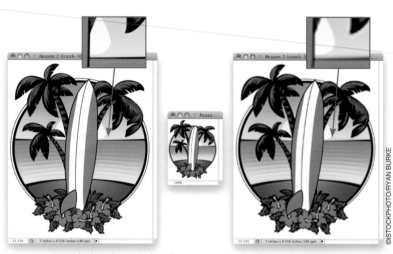

A regular layer loses quality when you resize it smaller then larger again

REASON 2B: SMART OBJECTS ARE RESIZABLE

However, if the layer that you're resizing is a Smart Object layer, then it will remain crisp even though you're resizing it.

A Smart Object layer remains crisp when you resize it smaller then larger again

REASON 3A: SMART OBJECTS ARE REPLACEABLE

Another really cool feature of Smart Objects is that they're replaceable. Here's what it means: Let's say that you take the time to create a custom picture package layout with a single photo. Chances are you'd be duplicating, resizing, and moving several copies of the layers all over the place. Then you print it off and life is good. Now you come to the next project and want to use the same layout, but with a different photo. Without Smart Objects, you'd have to go back and change each and every layer to a different photo.

REASON 3B: SMART OBJECTS ARE REPLACEABLE

With Smart Objects layers, you just select one of the layers, click the Layer menu and choose Smart Objects>Replace Contents. Choose a different photo and all of the photos will be replaced at once, as seen here. Sweet!!!

Another really cool feature of Smart Objects is they let you work with vector artwork directly from Illustrator. Say you place a graphic, which was created in Illustrator, in your image. Then you later decide you want to change some aspect of that graphic—be it color or shape. Without Smart Objects, you'd have to delete your layers and start over again after you change the graphic in Illustrator.

Note: In Chapter 10, we'll go over how to make the image appear as if it's actually on the t-shirt and wraps around the folds of the shirt.

©ISTOCKPHOTO/SUMNERS GRAPHICS INC.

With Smart Object layers, all you have to do is double-click on the graphic layer in Photoshop. It knows that the artwork originated in Illustrator and will open it in Illustrator automatically. Then you make your changes, save the file, and Photoshop will automatically update each instance of the graphic on any Smart Object layers.

REASON 5A: SMART OBJECTS REMEMBER WHEN THEY'RE RAW FILES

MATT KLOSKOWSKI

Let's say you're working on a RAW photo in Camera Raw. Go about making your exposure and white balance changes as normal. But when you're done, if you press-and-hold the Shift key, you'll see the Open Image button (at the bottom right) changes to Open Object. If you click it, the photo automatically opens in Photoshop as a Smart Object layer.

REASON 5B: SMART OBJECTS REMEMBER WHEN THEY'RE RAW FILES

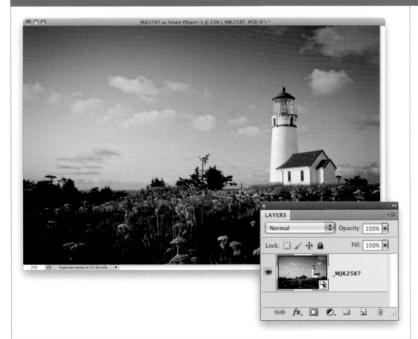

Here's where having a RAW photo as a Smart Object layer becomes really useful: Let's say you'd like to re-edit the RAW settings at some point. All you have to do is double-click on the Smart Object layer in the Layers panel and Photoshop will bring you right back to Camera Raw. Camera Raw will automatically remember all of your settings from before. Now, you can make your changes and click OK. Camera Raw will save the settings and update your photo back in Photoshop (I've converted this photo to black and white).

Note: Don't forget to check out the double-processing technique later in this chapter to see how Smart Objects can help when you're editing your photos in Photoshop.

DESIGNING TEMPLATES WITH SMART OBJECTS

THE TEMPLATE DESIGNS YOU CAN START BUILDING WITH SMART OBJECT LAYERS ARE AMAZING

Let's face it. The designs you can create with Smart Object layers are not, from a visual aspect, any different from what you could create with regular layers. However, this is one of those tutorials that will blow your mind from an automation standpoint. The way that Smart Object layers can be used to create reusable templates is way cool and truly showcases the power of Smart Objects.

STEP 1: OPEN A PHOTO THAT WILL BE THE MAIN IMAGE FOR AN ALBUM PAGE

Open the main photo for this design. You'll see that the project here works great for creating reusable album pages. These files can be saved and opened later to easily swap out the photo. If you want to try this with the wedding image I used here, you can download it from the website I talked about in the book's introduction.

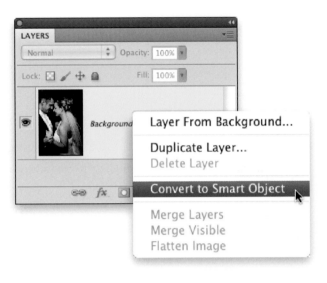

Start out by turning the Background layer into a Smart Object. In the last tutorial we just used File>Open as Smart Object, but you can turn any layer into a Smart Object, even after it's open. Just Right-click on the layer and choose Convert to Smart Object. Nothing will change visually in the image, but you'll now see the little Smart Object icon on the layer thumbnail in the Layers panel and the Background layer will be renamed "Layer 0."

Press Command-J (PC: Ctrl-J) to duplicate the Smart Object layer, so now you have two Smart Object layers.

STEP 4: MAKE A SQUARE SELECTION AND ADD A LAYER MASK TO THE DUPLICATE LAYER

Select the Rectangular Marquee tool (M) and make a square selection near the top right of the image. Make sure the duplicate copy of the Smart Object layer is the selected layer. Then click on the Add Layer Mask icon at the bottom of the Layers panel to turn the selection into a layer mask.

STEP 5: USE FREE TRANSFORM TO RESIZE THE PHOTO TO BETTER FIT INTO THE VISIBLE SQUARE

Now let's resize the Smart Object layer to make it fit into the square area better. Click on the Smart Object image thumbnail in the Layers panel, and then click on the link icon in between the image thumbnail and layer mask (this unlinks the image and mask, allowing you to move and resize the image on its own). Click the Edit menu and choose Free Transform. Press-and-hold the Shift key and drag one of the corner points inward to reduce the size of the photo. Resize it enough so you can still fill the square with the bride. Move your cursor inside the Free Transform bounding box to move it around, then press the Return (PC: Enter) key to commit your transformation.

STEP 6: REPEAT STEPS 3–5 TWO MORE TIMES. PLACE THE DUPLICATES EVENLY ALONG THE RIGHT SIDE

Repeat Steps 3–5 twice. Duplicate the original Smart Object layer, make a selection, add a layer mask, and use Free Transform to reposition each one. Try to vary each photo so it showcases a different part of the photo—almost making it look like there are three different photos, even though they're actually the same one. When you make your selections, arrange them evenly along the right side of the image.

Note: I thought the image looked better flipped for the middle and bottom squares, so when I was transforming them, I went to the Edit menu and chose Transform> Flip Horizontal.

STEP 7: ADD DROP SHADOW, STROKE, AND INNER GLOW LAYER STYLES

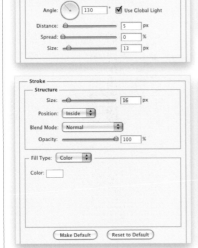

Double-click one of the small, square Smart Object layers you just created to open the Layer Style dialog. Add a Drop Shadow layer style, drop the Opacity to 50%, the Distance to 5, and increase the Size to 13. Then add an Inner Glow layer style, changing the color swatch to black, the Blend Mode pop-up menu to Multiply, and lowering the Opacity to 60. Finally, add a Stroke layer style. Set the Size to 16 px, Position to Inside, and set the Color to white. Click OK when you're done.

Copy the layer style you just added to the other two square layers. To do this, press-and-hold the Option (PC: Alt) key and click-and-drag the layer style (*fx*) icon onto the other two layers to duplicate the three layer styles on those layers.

Click once on the bottom layer (the original Smart Object layer). Then, in the Adjustments panel (Window>Adjustments), click on the Levels icon (the second one from the left in the first row) to create a Levels adjustment layer. In the Levels options, drag the black Output Levels slider to 118 to screen the background photo and make it appear lighter than everything else.

STEP 10: APPLY A GAUSSIAN BLUR FILTER ON THE BACKGROUND PHOTO

Click back on the bottom layer and let's add a blur to it to enhance its effect as a background design element and not a major player in the whole image. Since the layer is a Smart Object layer, we can take advantage of Smart Filters—you know, the kind you can always come back and change. So, click the Filter menu and choose Blur> Gaussian Blur. Enter a setting of 3 pixels and click OK. Then take a look at the layer in the Layers panel. You'll see the Smart Filters sublayer appear right under it. We don't need to edit it right now, but we will in a moment and you'll see how easy it is.

STEP 11: ADD A WHITE RECTANGLE SHAPE LAYER ON THE LEFT

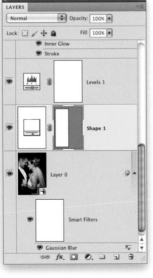

We're just about done. Now select the Rectangle tool (the Shape tool, not the Marquee tool; press U to get it). Press D, then X to set your Foreground color to white and draw a large rectangle over the left side of the image.

STEP 12: ADD A STROKE LAYER STYLE. CHANGE THE COLOR TO BLACK. REDUCE THE FILL OPACITY

Double-click the Shape layer you just created and add a Stroke layer style. Change the Size to 2 px and the Color to black. Click OK to add the style and close the Layer Style dialog. Then, reduce the Fill of the layer (at the top right of the Layers panel) to 30%. This leaves the Stroke layer style at full opacity, but reduces the white from the layer so you can see through it.

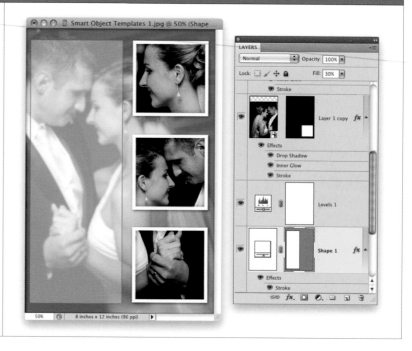

STEP 13: ADD SOME TEXT ON TOP OF THE RECTANGLE

Select the Type tool (T). Click-and-drag inside the white rectangle to create a large text box. Then add some text. I used Edwardian Script for the font and set the font size to 41 pt.

TIP: To increase the space between each line of text, go into the Character panel (Window>Character) and increase the leading amount to 90 pt.

STEP 14: REPLACE ANY ONE OF THE SMART OBJECT LAYERS AND THEY WILL ALL BE REPLACED

Now for the icing on the cake. What happens when the next project comes along and you have a photo of another couple? Just save this image as a PSD file. Then reopen it when the next project comes along. Click on any of the Smart Object layers, then click the Layer menu and choose Smart Objects>Replace Contents. Find another photo of similar size and orientation and click Place. All four photos are replaced. The size differences are maintained in each of them. The masks stay put. The layer styles carry over and even the Gaussian Blur is applied to the new photo. (You can applaud now.)

STEP 15: ADJUST THE POSITION OF ANY PHOTOS AND THE GAUSSIAN BLUR SMART FILTER

The thing that really brings this over the top is that you can move or resize any of the three smaller photos (remember, they're Smart Objects, so you can resize them without losing image quality). So if the new photo doesn't match perfectly, you can change it. Also, look at the Gaussian Blur Smart Filters sublayer. In the new photo it appears too blurry. No problem. Just double-click on Gaussian Blur and adjust the setting. I dropped it down to 2 pixels here and clicked OK. Now that is one heck of a flexible Photoshop document!

DOUBLE PROCESSING YOUR PHOTOS

WHEN YOU WISH YOU HAD MULTIPLE EXPOSURES, BUT YOU ONLY HAVE ONE

One of the most-used techniques for me, when it comes to Smart Object layers, is the double-processing technique. It comes in really handy when you have a photo where one area looks properly exposed, but another area looks too dark or too bright (kinda like our Combining Multiple Exposures tutorial in Chapter 6). When we take the photo, our eyes see everything that's there, but our camera doesn't. Sure, it's helpful to take two separate photos with different exposure settings to capture all the parts of the photo, but with Smart Objects, you'll see you can get just as good a result with one photo.

STEP 1: OPEN AND ADJUST A RAW PHOTO IN CAMERA RAW

Open a RAW photo in Camera Raw. Here, you can see the foreground looks great (which is what I exposed this photo for), but I had to make a decision in-camera to capture that foreground knowing the sky was going to be too bright. When standing there, I could see everything just fine. But our cameras simply don't capture what we see. So, first things first, go ahead and make your Camera Raw adjustments to the photo (like White Balance, Exposure, Sharpening, Vibrance, etc.). Do the normal things you'd do to the image, but only look at the foreground when you're doing this. Forget about the sky for now.

MATT KLOSKOWSKI

STEP 2: PRESS-AND-HOLD THE SHIFT KEY TO OPEN THE PHOTO IN PHOTOSHOP AS A SMART OBJECT

I mentioned in the first tutorial of this chapter that you can open your photos as Smart Objects in Photoshop from Camera Raw. Just press-and-hold the Shift key and you'll notice the Open Image button (at the bottom right) changes to Open Object. Click on Open Object and your photo automatically opens in Photoshop as a Smart Object layer.

STEP 3: DUPLICATE THE SMART OBJECT LAYER

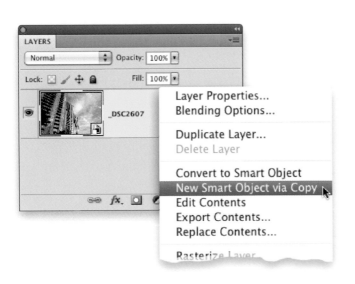

Let's make a copy of this layer. You can't just use the regular Layer>Duplicate Layer command, though, because that duplicate would be linked to the original and our double-processing technique won't work. Instead, go to the Layers panel and Right-click on the Smart Object layer, then choose New Smart Object via Copy. This makes a new copy of the Smart Object layer and it lets us do all of the cool things we're about to do—but it's not linked to the original layer anymore.

STEP 4: EDIT THE SMART OBJECT COPY LAYER IN CAMERA RAW

Now, we'll go back to Camera Raw and adjust the image so the sky looks good. Double-click the Smart Object copy (the top layer). It'll go straight into Camera Raw, because Photoshop knows it was a RAW file and that you've already edited it (remember, it's "smart"). Camera Raw automatically opens with the same settings you applied back in Step 1. This time, edit your photo so the sky looks good. That'll probably involve reducing the Exposure setting and maybe even increasing the Recovery slider to bring down the highlights. I also increased the Clarity and Vibrance settings. Now, your foreground will look like total crap. Don't worry. We only care about the sky this time. Click OK when you're done to return to Photoshop.

STEP 5: BACK IN PHOTOSHOP, YOU'LL NOW HAVE TWO VERSIONS OF THE SAME PHOTO

When you return to Photoshop, you'll now have two different versions (layers) of your photo. The top layer will be the one where the sky looks good and the bottom layer will be the one where the foreground looks good. You won't see the bottom layer, though, because the top layer covers it. But, we'll take care of that next.

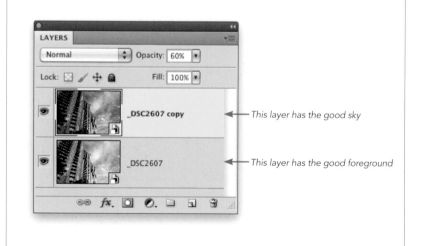

This layer has the good sky

This layer has the good foreground

STEP 6: MAKE A SELECTION ON THE TOP LAYER OF THE AREA YOU WANT TO KEEP

All we need to do to get the best of both worlds is to make a selection and add a mask. Grab the Quick Selection tool (W) and create a selection over the area of the photo that you want to keep. In this example, we want to keep the sky, so I'm creating a selection over the entire sky.

STEP 7: ADD A LAYER MASK TO REVEAL THE OTHER GOOD PARTS OF THE PHOTO

Finally, click the Add Layer Mask icon at the bottom of the Layers panel. The layer mask automatically hides whatever was not selected on that top layer (the foreground in this case), but it keeps the sky visible. So, now we have the best of both worlds—we can see the good sky from the top layer and the good foreground from the bottom one. And if you want to re-edit either of those to make them brighter or darker, just double-click its Smart Object thumbnail and that photo will reopen in Camera Raw. You can make your changes and when you return to Photoshop, that layer will be updated (but your layer mask will still be there, so you still only see the parts of the photo that you want to).

Before

After

HOW DO I...

OPEN AN IMAGE AS A SMART OBJECT?

Click the File menu and choose Open as Smart Object. Find the image you want to open and click on the Open button. That image will show up just like normal in the Layers panel, but it will be a Smart Object layer instead.

PLACE AN IMAGE INTO AN ALREADY OPEN IMAGE AS A SMART OBJECT?

Click the File menu and choose Place. Navigate to your image and click on the Place button. The placed image will show up as a Smart Object in your image.

CONVERT A REGULAR LAYER INTO A SMART OBJECT?

You can always go under the Layer menu to Smart Objects>Convert to Smart Object. But, my favorite way is to Right-click on the layer and choose Convert to Smart Object, instead. It's a lot faster.

GIVE A LAYER THE ABILITY TO USE SMART FILTERS?

Smart Filters will only work on Smart Object layers, so convert your layer to a Smart Object before you apply the filter to it (see above). Then, all of the filters you add to that layer will show up as Smart Filters, and will be completely editable.

REPLACE A SMART OBJECT?

To replace a Smart Object on one layer with another image, just click the Layer menu and choose Smart Objects>Replace Contents.

SAVE MY LAYERS SO I CAN USE THEM IN ANOTHER ADOBE CREATIVE SUITE PROGRAM?

All you need to do is make sure you save your file as a Photoshop PSD file. That will give you the greatest compatibility with other Adobe Creative Suite programs. Oh yeah, if the Maximize Compatibility dialog ever pops up when you're saving your images, make sure you always choose to maximize the compatibility. That'll help make sure your images work well with other programs.

CHAPTER TEN

ADVANCED LAYER BLENDING AND COMPOSITING

This chapter is brand new to this version of the book. I realized that I still had a few tutorials that I really wanted to include. But they just didn't seem to fit in other chapters. Essentially, the tutorials fit into a theme of blending, placing, and compositing things into images where they don't really belong. Between the improved selection capabilities of Photoshop CS5 and the blending options that have been around for years, there are plenty of ways to move part of one image into another and make it look realistic. I have to warn you, though, it's an advanced chapter. It moves fast. I'm assuming you've read and have a good grasp of everything we've done so far in the book (masking, selections, blending, adjustments). That said, let's roll up our sleeves and dive in.

REPLACING A PERSON'S BACKGROUND

MOVING SOMEONE TO A DIFFERENT BACKGROUND IS ONE OF THE MOST POWERFUL THINGS TO DO WITH LAYERS

True story: I've been practicing taekwondo for a while now and, last year, I took some photos of my instructors. These are two of the nicest and most talented people I know (sorry, I had to suck up for a second so they don't kick my butt). Seriously, they are! (Not sucking up anymore, it's true.) Anyway, I remember showing them the photos and they were really appreciative. They were nice portraits and everyone liked them. But a few months later, I was experimenting with some new techniques and I decided to take one of the photos and place it on a different background. Within a few minutes, the photo was totally transformed. But what I remember most was the reaction when I showed them. The photo that got a "Thanks, Matt, these are great. We really appreciate it" a few months earlier, now got a "Wow! Oh my God! This is the coolest photo of me ever!" reaction. Same photo. Just a different background. Let's take a look at exactly what I did.

STEP 1: OPEN THE TWO PHOTOS AND MOVE THE PERSON ONTO THEIR NEW BACKGROUND

Start out by opening the two photos you'll be working with. Here's a photo of Master David Kowkabany (sixth-degree black belt, and a guy who regularly sees to it that I have zero energy left after leaving his class), and a photo of a background I found on Fotolia.com while searching for the word "abandoned." Go ahead and copy-and-paste the photo of the person over onto the new background. Then go to Edit>Free Transform to make sure they fit into the area you're working with. Press-and-hold the Shift key while you resize the image to keep it proportional.

STEP 2: USE THE QUICK SELECTION TOOL TO MAKE A SELECTION OF THE PERSON

Click on the layer of the person whose background you need to remove. Use the Quick Selection tool (W) to paint inside the person to make a selection. It's worth taking some time to zoom in and get the selection right (press Z to get the Zoom tool). Don't forget you can change the size of the brush to get those small areas. You can also press-and-hold the Option (PC: Alt) key to remove any areas that are accidentally selected.

Note: Don't forget about the selection basics tutorial online at www.kelbytraining.com/book /layerscs5.

STEP 3: ADD A LAYER MASK. USE THE REFINE MASK DIALOG TO REFINE THE ORIGINAL SELECTION

Now that we have a selection, let's add a mask to it. Remember how masks work: when you already have a selection created, they keep whatever is selected and hide whatever is not. So, click on the Add Layer Mask icon at the bottom of the Layers panel to add a layer mask to the layer and it'll automatically hide the background. We'll need to refine the edge a little, so go to the Masks panel (Window>Masks) and click the Mask Edge button. Turn on the Smart Radius checkbox and drag the Radius slider to around 10 pixels. You can also use the Refine Radius tool (on the left side of the dialog) to brush around any edges that didn't get selected well the first time. Click OK when you're done.

STEP 4: ADJUST THE SKIN COLOR OF THE PERSON TO MATCH THE BACKGROUND

A telltale sign that you've placed someone into a different background is the color of the light. The original photo was taken in a studio (with flash) and has a very cool/blue feel to it, while the background I've pasted him onto has a warm feel to it. A great way to fix this is with a Photo Filter adjustment. Go to the Adjustments panel and click on the Photo Filter icon (the little camera). Use the default warming filter, and move the Density slider to around 35%–40%. You'll notice the adjustment affects the entire image, though. So, just click on the Clip to Layer icon (the third icon from the left) at the bottom of the Adjustments panel to restrict the adjustment to only the layer below it.

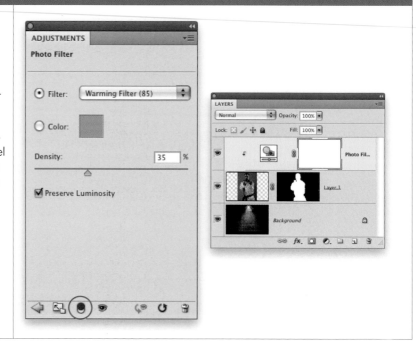

STEP 5: PAINT AT 50% OPACITY ON THE LAYER MASK TO REDUCE THE PHOTO FILTER EFFECT

The Photo Filter adjustment layer warmed up his skin tone, but it also made his uniform too warm. We can fix that using the adjustment layer's mask, so select the Brush tool (B) and, up in the Options Bar, set its Opacity to 50%. Make sure your Foreground color is set to black, and paint over just his uniform.

STEP 6: ADJUST THE LIGHTING OF THE PERSON TO MATCH THE IMAGE

Another sign of Photoshop fakeness is the overall brightness of the person. If they look too bright or too dark, then try using a Curves adjustment layer and drag the center of the curve up or down, depending on how bright or dark you need to make them compared to the background. Again, this will affect the entire image, so click on that Clip to Layer icon at the bottom of the Adjustments panel to keep the effects on the portrait layer only. Since this darkens both his skin and uniform (and I only wanted to darken the uniform), paint with a black brush on the layer mask over the face and hands to hide the effects of the Curves adjustment layer.

STEP 7: MERGE THE LAYERS TOGETHER TO MAKE THINGS EASIER TO WORK WITH

Since we're starting to build up our layers here, it's easier to merge them into one so we can keep track of them better. But we won't flatten everything; we'll just create a flattened version on top. Click on the topmost layer in the Layers panel, then press Command-Option-Shift-E (PC: Ctrl-Alt-Shift-E) to create a flattened copy at the top of the layer stack.

STEP 8: APPLY AN EDGY LOOK TO THE PERSON WITH THE HIGH PASS FILTER

Let's create an edgy look for the portrait to accentuate the highlights and shadows on his face and uniform and make the image more dramatic. I've got a Photoshop way to do this and a third-party plugin way (that I prefer). We'll look at Photoshop first: Click on the portrait layer, and press Command-J (PC: Ctrl-J) to duplicate it. Drag it above the merged layer from the previous step. Go to Filter>Other>High Pass and adjust the Radius setting so most of the portrait looks gray, but you can see some details of the highlights and shadows. Each photo is different, but a setting of 8 pixels is good here. Click OK, then change the layer blend mode to Soft Light to hide the gray and keep the edgy, detailed look.

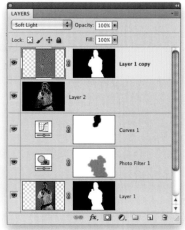

STEP 9: MY SECRET WEAPON FOR SPECIAL EFFECTS

I just showed you the Photoshop way to do this, but you wanna know the truth? I have a secret weapon for special effects. I use it all the time and rarely ever do them manually in Photoshop. This particular one for portraits is from Topaz Labs and it's called Topaz Adjust. It's got a ton of filters. One of them is called "Detail – Strong," and it does a way better job (and much faster) than anything we can do in Photoshop. I also lowered the layer's Opacity to 80% because it was a little too strong. Okay, so you can't get mad at me. I gave you the free Photoshop way to do it. I'm just being honest. This is what I actually use for my professional work. Download a free demo at www.topazlabs.com to check it out.

STEP 10: SOFTEN SOME OF THE HARSH EFFECTS ON THE FACE

Because of the lighting in this photo, the edge effect looks good in most areas. However, it accentuated some of the shadows on his face. If you recall from Chapter 7 (Retouching with Layers), we can use the same technique we used for removing blemishes and wrinkles to remove some of the darker areas. So, click on the Create a New Layer icon at the bottom of the Layers panel, and use the Healing Brush (press Shift-J until you have it), with the Sample All Layers option chosen in the Options Bar, to soften some of those dark areas under his eyes and on his forehead. Then reduce the opacity to about 50% to blend the adjustments with the original.

STEP 11: SPICE UP THE BACKGROUND

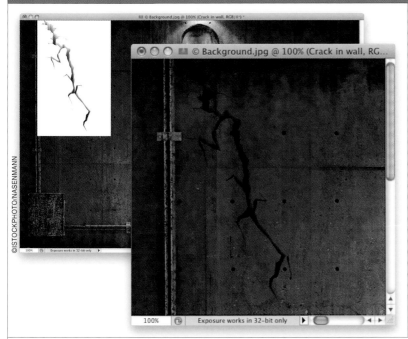

To spice up the background a bit, I've copied-and-pasted another image on top of it. It's supposed to be a crack in the earth, but by changing the blend mode to Multiply, it hides the white and makes for a nice effect on our wall. I even copied that layer and used another one on the right side of the wall, too.

STEP 12: ADD A SYMBOL TO THE WALL ON THE BACKGROUND

Hide the portrait layers for a minute by clicking on the Eye icons to the left of the their thumbnails. Now, click on the merged layer below the High Pass or Topaz Adjust filter layer. Open the Asian symbol image for this tutorial and copy-and-paste it into this image (it should appear on a layer right below the filter layer). Use the Move tool to move it into the center area of the image.

STEP 13: ADD LAYER STYLES TO MAKE IT LOOK CARVED INTO THE WALL

Of course, it doesn't look so good as just a black symbol, so we're going to use some layer styles to make it look like it's carved into the wall. Double-click the layer to open the Layer Style dialog. Click on the Bevel and Emboss and Inner Glow styles on the left and use the settings you see here.

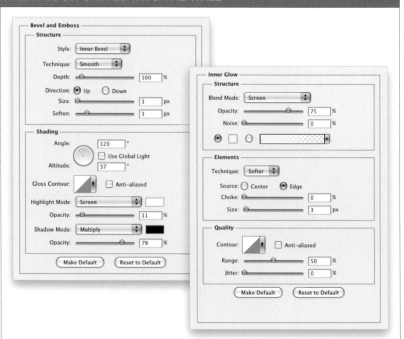

STEP 14: ADJUST THE FILL OPACITY TO REVEAL THE LAYER STYLES

Now add an Inner Shadow layer style. The main thing to keep in mind is the lighting angle. Look at the background. There's light coming from the top middle, so make sure all lighting sources for your styles come from above and cast their effect downward (especially the Inner Shadow). The symbol doesn't yet look like it's carved into the wall, but here's the key: Fill Opacity. We used it in Chapter 8 to create a watermark. Click on Blending Options at the top left of the Layer Style dialog. Reduce the Fill Opacity setting to 0. This hides the black from the symbol, but leaves all of the layer styles on the layer, which is what gives it that carved-in look. Click OK when you're done.

STEP 15: TURN THE PORTRAIT LAYERS BACK ON AND FINISH WITH A LAYER MASK

Once you're finished with the layer styles, turn your portrait layers back on by clicking where their Eye icons used to be. You'll see that part of the Asian symbol still shows up over him. That's an easy fix with a layer mask. Start by Command-clicking (PC: Ctrl-clicking) on the filter layer's mask to create a selection around him. Then, click on the Asian symbol layer to make it active, and Option-click (PC: Alt-click) on the Add Layer Mask icon at the bottom of the Layers panel to create a layer mask with the selection filled with black, so it hides that part of the Asian symbol instead of showing it.

ADVANCED LAYER BLENDING

THERE'S ONE MORE ASPECT OF LAYER BLENDING THAT WE HAVEN'T SEEN YET

There's one area of blending layers that we haven't looked at yet: the Blend If sliders in Blending Options. Trust me, this is *way* different than anything you've seen before. See, blend modes fade parts of your image based on the colors in them, but you really don't have any control over what gets blended. There's a preset formula for a blend mode and it will always follow that formula. The Blend If sliders, on the other hand, let you control exactly which parts of the photo get blended.

STEP 1: OPEN TWO IMAGES THAT YOU'D LIKE TO BLEND TOGETHER

Open two images that you'd like to blend together. Here, we'll use a photo of a couple and a template with a place to insert a photo. We want to blend the couple into the black area of the template (but inside of the white border). No sweat, right? But, look closely. There's some sand over the black area, and let me tell ya, that would make for a really nasty selection. Instead, we'll use a more advanced section of the Layer Style dialog that does the work for us.

STEP 2: MOVE THE PHOTO OF THE COUPLE INTO THE SAME DOCUMENT AS THE BEACH TEMPLATE

To kick things off, get the Move tool (V) and click-and-drag the photo of the couple into the same document as the beach template. Go to Edit>Free Transform, then move and rotate it to position it over the black area (you can always lower the layer's opacity at the top right of the Layers panel to help you determine where to place it). It doesn't have to be perfect, but you'll want to get it into the ballpark of where it'll end up.

STEP 3: OPEN THE BLENDING OPTIONS

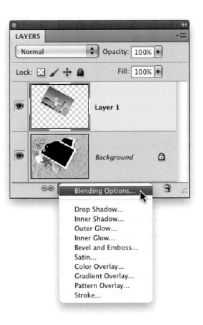

To merge these two images together, we'll use the Layers panel's Blending Options layer style. Click on the Add a Layer Style icon at the bottom of the Layers panel and choose Blending Options from the pop-up menu.

TIP: You can also double-click on the layer as a shortcut to open the Blending Options section of the Layer Style dialog.

STEP 4: EXPERIMENT WITH THE TOP BLEND IF SLIDER

Before we totally jump in, let's take a look at the area we'll be working with. It's the Blend If section at the bottom of the dialog. Try experimenting with the top sliders under This Layer. Drag the black slider toward the right. See, the top Blend If slider works on the current layer (remember, This Layer). When you drag the black slider knob, it removes all of the dark areas on the current layer and reveals the layer below (which is just black here). In this case, that means the man's hair would be removed first, since it's really dark, then the shadows on the ground and the green hills in the background.

STEP 5: EXPERIMENT SOME MORE WITH THE TOP BLEND IF SLIDER

The white slider knob on the right side works the same way, but removes the white, or brightest, areas first. In our example, that means the bride's dress, the groom's suit, waves on the beach, and the sand would be among the first things to go. Again, you'll see whatever is under them in the Layers panel, which is just black in this case. The further you drag to the left, the more area you tell Photoshop to blend (or hide).

STEP 6: WHAT THE HECK IS GOING ON?

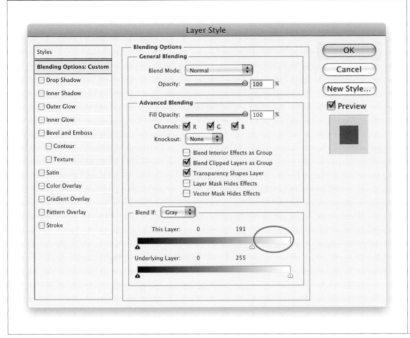

All right, if you're one of those people who has to know how and why this is happening, here's the deal: the Blend If sliders tell Photoshop to blend certain color values if a layer's values fall within a certain range. In the example in the previous step, we told Photoshop to blend the top layer with the couple on it, if any color values from this layer (which is the one we've selected in the Layers panel) fall between 191 and 255. Remember, 191 is where we set the slider. If you look at the dialog here, you'll see the colors that are circled are the ones blended (mostly whites and even some light shades of gray). That's why the wedding dress was the first to blend away.

STEP 7: NOW WORK WITH THE BOTTOM BLEND IF SLIDER—UNDERLYING LAYER

The Underlying Layer Blend If slider works nearly the same, but instead of blending away (or hiding) areas of the top layer, it reveals areas of the underlying layer. If you move the black slider knob toward the right, you'll tell Photoshop to show you all parts of the underlying layer that are black (which is just about everything but the sand). This is actually the opposite of what we want, though.

Now try moving the white Underlying Layer Blend If slider knob toward the left (this is cool). Watch what happens as you drag it over. First off, any part of the photo that extended over the white border disappears. So we didn't even have to make a selection to get the photo into the border. But, let's face it. The sand is really what we're worried about. Well, as you drag the slider further toward the left to around 70, the parts of the photo over the sand disappear. Even the small grains of sand show up perfectly.

Ready for the kicker? The thing that brings this all together? If you zoom in (press Z to get the Zoom tool), you'll see the black edges of the background around the tiny grains of sand. It's the one telltale sign that we've "faked" this image. To fix it, press-and-hold the Option (PC: Alt) key and click-and-drag the white Underlying Layer slider knob to the right. This splits the knob and tells Photoshop to fade any colors between the two ends of it. Take the right half of the knob over to 155 or so, and you'll see the black edges disappear, so the grains of sand look like they're lying on the photo. Click OK and you're done. Sweet, huh? Best of all, no painful selections were made in this process.

WRAPPING GRAPHICS ON UNEVEN SURFACES

USING LAYERS AND A VERY SPECIALIZED FILTER, YOU CAN WRAP GRAPHICS AROUND THE FOLDS OF CLOTHING

Back in Chapter 9, one of the examples of Smart Objects showed an image wrapped onto a t-shirt. But, it wasn't just pasted on the t-shirt. I used a few layer-related blending tricks and a filter to make it appear that way. To make it convincing, the graphic needs to bend where the folds are, and it also needs to show some of the shadows and highlights from the t-shirt itself. Let's take a look at how it was done.

STEP 1: OPEN THE IMAGE YOU WANT TO WRAP A GRAPHIC ONTO

Start out by opening the image that you want to wrap a graphic onto. In our example, I'll use a photo of a t-shirt. This would come in really handy if you were selling t-shirts (or other items), but you didn't have an actual photo of the t-shirt with the printed graphic on it. Sure, you could just show a picture of the artwork and people could imagine what it would look like on a t-shirt, but this is much more convincing.

STEP 2: REMOVE THE COLOR FROM THE IMAGE AND INCREASE ITS CONTRAST

In order for this to work, we need to create what's called a texture map that emphasizes the folds in the t-shirt. So go to the Image menu and choose Duplicate. We'll need a copy of our original image to work with at first. Then go to Image>Adjustments>Desaturate to remove all of the color from the t-shirt. Once the color is gone, we need to add some contrast to the image. Go to Image>Adjustments> Levels (no need for an adjustment layer here), and bring both the black and white Input Levels sliders toward the center to create a really contrasty look to the t-shirt. Click OK when you're done.

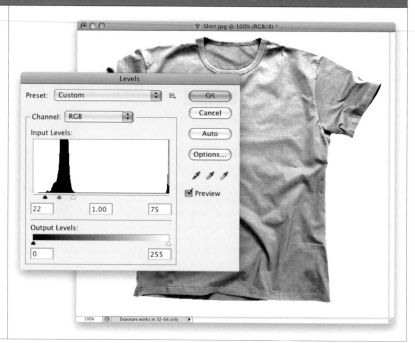

STEP 3: BLUR THE IMAGE TO SMOOTH THE DETAILS

Since the t-shirt looks really con-strasty, we need to smooth it out a little. We can do that with a blur filter. Go to Filter>Blur>Gaussian Blur and apply enough blur so that the folds on the t-shirt look smooth, but are still very visible. It's going to differ for every image, but a setting of 4 pixels worked well for me here. Click OK when you're done.

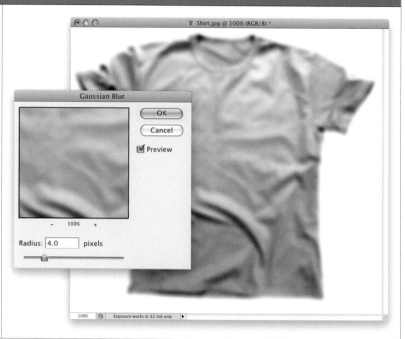

STEP 4: SAVE AS A PSD

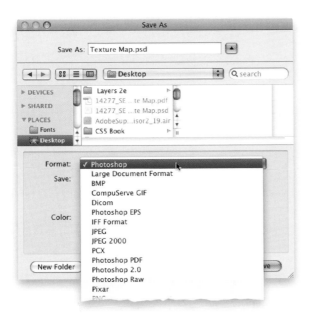

Go to File>Save As (or press Command-Shift-S [PC: Ctrl-Shift-S]), and save this image to your desktop as a PSD file. I usually name mine "Texture Map.psd," just so I know it's a texture map and I can delete it later on. When you're done, you can close the texture map image, since we don't need it open anymore.

STEP 5: OPEN THE GRAPHIC AND PLACE IT ON A LAYER ABOVE THE SHIRT

Re-open the original t-shirt image, and also open the graphic that you want to place onto the t-shirt. Copy-and-paste that graphic (the surfboard and palm trees here) into your t-shirt image. You should only have two layers at this point: the t-shirt layer at the bottom, and the graphic you want to blend onto it on the top layer.

STEP 6: APPLY THE DISPLACE FILTER

We're going to use a filter to make the graphic appear as if it's wrapped onto the t-shirt. I've never used this filter for anything else, so it's pretty much a one-trick pony. But it works. Go to Filter>Distort>Displace. The default settings work fine, so click OK, and you'll see another dialog asking you to Choose a Displacement Map (this is the only filter that gives you two dialogs). Just navigate to the PSD that you saved in Step 4, click on it, and choose Open to apply the filter. You'll see the graphic becomes somewhat distorted and wavy around the folds of the shirt, based on the black-and-white version of the t-shirt we applied to it.

STEP 7: CHANGE THE BLENDING OPTIONS

Okay, the image is kinda flat the way it looks right now. So, to finish things off, double-click on the layer to go into the Blending Options section of the Layer Style dialog (just like we did in the previous tutorial). In the Underlaying Layer Blend If slider, press-and-hold the Option (PC: Alt) key and click-and-drag the black slider knob toward the middle to split it. As you drag it, you'll start to see the folds from the shirt appear through the image we just wrapped on it. Click OK when you're done.

Here's a side-by-side comparison of the image on the shirt with no displacement or blending applied and the one with the effect. You can see that the After image is a lot more convincing than the Before.

TIP: I didn't have to do it on this image, but sometimes changing the layer's blend mode to Multiply or Overlay (or even Soft Light) works well, too. You have to experiment a little based on the pasted image, as well as what's under it.

Before: The graphic has just been copied-and-pasted onto the t-shirt

After: The Displace filter has been applied and the Blending Options Blend If sliders used to wrap and blend the graphic onto the t-shirt

USING LAYERS FOR LIGHTING AND SHADOWS

BY USING LAYERS, WE CAN NOT ONLY CHANGE A PERSON'S BACKGROUND, BUT ALSO THE SHADOWS AND LIGHTING AROUND THEM

We're gonna step it up a bit in this tutorial and really start to push layers to change the environment around a person. The earlier background tutorial in this chapter was a good first step in replacing a person's background, since we literally just put them on a different background. We didn't have to worry about perspective and lighting that much. But in this example, you'll see there's no way we can pull off the composite by just placing the person on a new background. The angle of light, location of light, shadows, and even the color of light will all affect how we pull this one off. Don't sweat it, though. Aside from a new blend mode (that we haven't worked with yet) and a new style of adjustment layer, all of the techniques use tools you've already seen.

STEP 1: OPEN THE BACKGROUND AND REMOVE ANY DISTRACTING OBJECTS

Start off by opening the background image you're going to be using. I chose an image I found on Fotolia.com. I didn't exactly know what I'd use it for when I found it, but I put it in my library knowing that it would make a great background some day. First, I duplicated the Background layer, then used the Spot Healing Brush (with the Content-Aware option turned on) to paint over a paint tray on the ground and remove it. It did a good job for a first pass, so I brushed over the area again and it helped. Then, I switched to the Clone Stamp tool to tidy it up a bit.

©FOTOLIA/SAMMYC

Part of lighting, shading, and compositing with layers is knowing the limits of what you can do. Having several portraits of this DJ (shot by a friend of mine, Russ Robinson), I knew there was no way the wrong perspective in the portrait would work for the background I had in mind. Photoshop can do a lot of things, but changing the perspective in which people were photographed isn't something it's really good at. So you have to start with a great photo, and I thought this photo of DJ Rob Analyze just had a really cool and dynamic feel to it. Once you have your photo, copy-and-paste it onto its new background.

Before we can do anything, we need to select him off of the white background. Start with the Quick Selection tool (W) and paint a selection in the portrait. Then, click the Add Layer Mask icon at the bottom of the Layers panel. Now, go to the Masks panel and click the Mask Edge button. Turn on the Smart Radius checkbox, and move the Radius slider to about 15 pixels. Then use the Refine Radius brush to brush around his hair, so most of it gets selected. Click OK when you're done.

STEP 4: PLACE THE PERSON ON A SEPARATE LAYER

If you see white fringe around the hair and body (which I do here), I've got a great tip for you: First, you'll need to put the selected person on their own layer. Command-click (PC: Ctrl-click) on the layer mask thumbnail to get a selection around the DJ. Then, click on the layer's image thumbnail to target it, and press Command-J (PC: Ctrl-J) to copy the DJ to his own layer. Hide the original layer with the mask (but don't delete it, in case you need it again). Everything looks the same, but the DJ is now on his own layer with no mask. I like to keep the mask, in case we need to change it, but there are some techniques that won't work if we have a layer mask on the layer.

STEP 5: REMOVE THE WHITE FRINGE

Okay, here's the really cool trick: Click on the DJ's layer (the one without the mask; it should be the top layer) to select it. Go to Layer>Matting>Remove White Matte (because the outline here is white). Almost instantly, the white fringe goes away and the edge looks way better. Compare it with the image in the previous step and you'll see what a big difference it makes.

TIP: If you had selected a person from a black background, then you'd use Layer>Matting>Remove Black Matte instead.

STEP 6: ADD A SHADOW LAYER BASED ON THE DIRECTION OF LIGHT

Since the selection looks good, it's time to start making it look real. The first thing is the lighting. He looks like he's floating on the ground without any shadows. You'll see there's a light source coming from back right, so it would cast a shadow to the front left. Command-click (PC: Ctrl-click) on the DJ layer's thumbnail to make a selection. Create a new layer under the DJ layer, go to Edit>Fill, and fill it with black. Then deselect. Go to Filter>Blur>Gaussian Blur and apply a 40-pixel blur to soften the shadow. Go to Edit>Transform>Flip Vertical, and use Free Transform to finesse the shadow into place. When you're done, try reducing the Opacity of the layer to around 60% to soften it even more.

STEP 7: ADD ANOTHER SHADOW DIRECTLY BELOW

Repeat Step 6, but this time, don't flip the shadow vertically. Instead, go into Free Transform and click-and-drag the top handle downward to place the shadow directly under the DJ. Move it around a little to get it into place under the knee on the right.

STEP 8: ADD A HARSH SHADOW LAYER BELOW THE FOOT AND KNEE

Let's add yet another shadow layer under the DJ. Add a blank layer and zoom in on his front foot. This is a key area to make look realistic because it's up front. Get the Brush tool, choose a small, soft-edged brush, and make sure your Foreground color is set to black. Brush around the edge of his shoe and the inside edge of his left knee (the one touching the ground) to add a slightly more harsh shadow. Shadows tend to spread out (like the previous ones) but under the feet (or any area touching the ground), you'll usually see a small, but dark shadow. When you're done, reduce the opacity of this layer to around 70%. Duplicate the layer and add a Gaussian blur to spread the shadow out, as well, then lower the layer's Opacity to around 25%.

STEP 9: GROUP THEM TOGETHER

The Layers panel is starting to grow, so let's keep things organized. Click on the topmost shadow layer and then Shift-click on the bottom one. Then, go to Layer>Group Layers to put them into a group (folder). Rename the group "Shadows," so you know what's in there.

TIP: Don't forget, you can always change the opacity of the group if you wanted to lighten or darken all of the shadow layers at once.

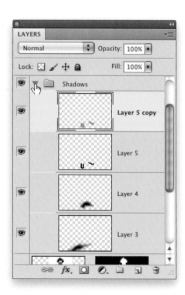

STEP 10: ADD A PHOTO FILTER TO MATCH THE SKIN TO THE BACKGROUND

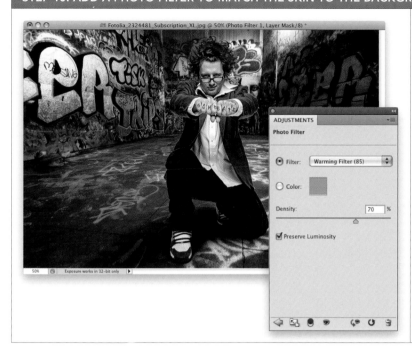

Now we need to match the lighting on the DJ to the scene that he's in. We'll do this with a Photo Filter layer. Click on the DJ layer, then go to the Adjustments panel and add a Photo Filter adjustment. Keep the default warming color (since the entire background is very warm), and change the Density to about 70%. That puts a warming color over the DJ to help match the scene that he's in. Before we move on, notice that adjustment layer is also warming the entire scene, because we're not masking or clipping the adjustment yet. No sweat. In Step 12, we'll see a killer new technique to help us focus the adjustment on only the DJ.

STEP 11: ADD A CURVES ADJUSTMENT LAYER TO DARKEN THE PERSON

Another issue we have is that the DJ is too bright compared to the scene he's in. Go ahead and add a Curves adjustment layer above the DJ, click on the center of the curve, and drag it downward to darken him a bit. Again, this darkens the whole scene, but we're going to take care of that next.

STEP 12: GROUP THE LAYERS TOGETHER AND CHANGE THE BLEND MODE TO NORMAL

We did something similar in the earlier background tutorial. There, we used clipping masks to "clip" an adjustment, so it only affected the layer below it. With multiple layers, there's an easier way to do this. Select the DJ layer, and the Photo Filter and Curves adjustment layers, and group them together. Click on the group and take a look at the blend mode. It's set to Pass Through, which means that any effects in the group "pass through" the group and affect anything below it (the background, in this case). We don't want that, though. We want to keep the effects in the group restricted to the group only, so change the blend mode to Normal. Now the adjustments only affect the DJ.

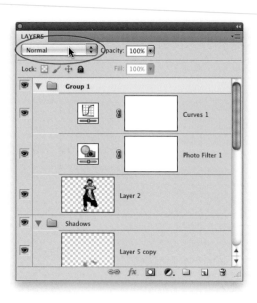

STEP 13: ADD A CONCERT-LIKE SPOTLIGHT TO THE BACKGROUND

I picked up this trick from my friend Calvin Hollywood—a very talented artist. We're going to spice up the existing light in the top right by adding a concert-like spotlight to it. Click on the group you just made, then click the Create New Adjustment Layer icon at the bottom of the Layers panel and choose Gradient. Change the Style to Angle and click on the gradient itself to edit it. In the Gradient Editor, for Gradient Type, choose Noise, for Color Model, choose HSB, and drag the white Saturation slider halfway to the left. Drag both the Hue sliders under the yellow area, so the gradient becomes yellow only (the color of the light). Lastly, click Randomize until you see something similar to what I have here.

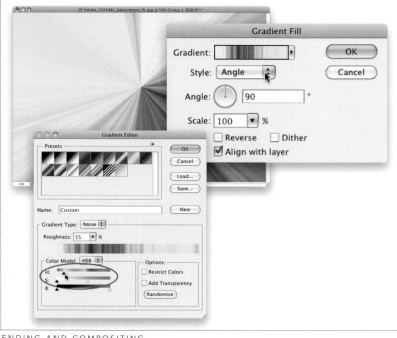

STEP 14: HIDE THE SPOTLIGHT FROM THE DJ LAYER

Click OK to close the Gradient Editor. Move your cursor over the image and reposition the center of the gradient to the top right. Click OK to close the Gradient Fill dialog. Now, if you change the blend mode to Screen, you'll drop out all of the black that was in the gradient and you'll be left with the rays of light. Command-Click (PC: Ctrl-Click) on the DJ layer's thumbnail to make a selection again, then click on the Gradient layer mask thumbnail and fill the selection with black to mask it from the DJ. Paint with black anywhere else you want to remove the lighting effect.

TIP: To reposition the center of the light source, double-click on the Gradient Fill layer's thumbnail.

STEP 15: COPY THE SPOTLIGHT AND MOVE IT INTO THE PORTRAIT GROUP FOR ACCENT LIGHTING

Since the spotlight is yellow, it would cast a yellow light onto the DJ, right? Duplicate the spotlight layer, and move it into the group with the DJ in it, but make it the top layer in the group. Click on the duplicate Gradient Fill layer's mask and go to Edit>Fill to fill it with black. Then zoom in on the image and paint with a small, white, soft-edged brush around the edges of the DJ, and in any areas you see white light hitting his clothes. In this example, I'm painting mostly on the outside right edges (since that's where the light is coming from), but also his knee and left shoulder. Try reducing the opacity of this layer to around 50% to soften the intensity of the light, as well.

STEP 16: ADD SOME SPECIAL EFFECTS TO THE PORTRAIT

In Step 8 of the earlier background tutorial, we added a contrasty edgy effect to the portrait. I think the portrait here can benefit from the same effect. I also showed you my preferred special effect for such portraits, using a third-party plug-in called Topaz Adjust (from Topaz Labs). Here, I duplicated the portrait layer, then added that same effect, using the Detail – Strong preset again.

STEP 17: ADD SOME SPECIAL EFFECTS TO THE BACKGROUND

The background can also use some grunginess on it, and you could use the same High Pass filter in Photoshop that we used in Step 8 of the earlier background tutorial for that (on a duplicate layer), but I like the Tonal Contrast filter from Nik Software's Color Efex Pro for my backgrounds. Again, don't get ticked at me. You have the recipe for the Photoshop method for this, but Nik's filter is really what I use, as you can see here.

STEP 18: ADD VIGNETTE

Finally, let's do some dodging and burning (mostly burning to add a light vignette to the background). I'm going to use the same technique from Chapter 6. Click on the topmost layer in the Layers panel and add a new blank layer above it. Go to Edit>Fill and fill it with 50% gray. Set the layer blend mode to Overlay. Now, grab the Brush tool and set your Foreground color to black and the tool's Opacity to 20%. Paint over the edges of the background to darken them a bit. It's a lot like a vignette, but you can control it, so you don't darken the DJ's head, but all of the other edges around him.

CREATING THE MAIN COVER IMAGE

LET'S DECONSTRUCT PART OF THE COVER IMAGE FOR THIS BOOK AND SEE HOW LAYERS PLAYED A KEY ROLE IN MAKING IT

In the last version of this book, our book designer (Jessica Maldonado) did a killer job on the cover. So much so, that I received a ton of questions asking how the cover was created. I couldn't help but kick myself for not including it as a tutorial in the book. After all, the cover was done with a bunch of layers, and most of the techniques are things that you learn right here in the book. So, this time around, I worked with Jessica (and Nicole Procunier, another one of our designers who created this image) to come up with a cover that I could also write about in the book. One more thing: We're only creating the main image from the cover here. If you want to see the entire cover design (wavy floating layers, background images, and all), I've put a video online for you at this book's download site mentioned in the introduction. In that video, we'll not only walk through what's in this tutorial, but the rest of the cover, too.

STEP 1: OPEN THE TWO MAIN IMAGES YOU'LL BE WORKING WITH AND COMBINE THEM

We're going to be using a few images for the cover, but let's start out with the two main ones. First, open the photo of the dancer, then open the grungy green background. Copy-and-paste the background image onto the dancer photo. Change the blend mode of the grungy green background to Overlay and reduce the opacity to 55%.

©FOTOLIA/ALEXANDER YAKOVLEV AND ISTOCKPHOTO/PETER ZELEI

STEP 2: COPY THE DANCER LAYER AND SELECT HER FROM THE BACKGROUND

Click on the dancer layer to make it active, press Command-J (PC: Ctrl-J) to make a duplicate, then click-and-drag it on top of the grungy background layer in the layer stack. Let's select her from the background with the Quick Selection tool (W), then click the Add Layer Mask icon at the bottom of the Layers panel. Now, go to the Masks panel and click the Mask Edge button. Turn on Smart Radius and move the slider to about 15 pixels. Use the Refine Radius brush to brush around her hair, so most of it gets selected. Don't worry if it's not perfect. It'll actually look better that way because of our background. Click OK when you're done.

STEP 3: DARKEN THE FLOOR, SO IT DOESN'T LOOK LIKE SHE'S FLOATING

Click on the grungy background layer to make it active and use the Rectangular Marquee tool (M) to make a selection of the bottom portion of the layer. Duplicate that portion of the layer, then click-and-drag it to the top of the layer stack. Change this new layer's blend mode to Multiply and reduce its opacity to around 25%. This gives her something to stand on, so it doesn't look like she's floating.

Go to the Adjustments panel and add a Hue/Saturation adjustment layer. Drag the Hue slider to +28 to add a little more blue to the background. Don't forget, you could change the color to anything here. You could also drag the Saturation slider toward the left to desaturate the color if you wanted. Gray actually looks pretty good here, too.

Since the Hue/Saturation adjustment layer affects the entire image right now, we need to add a layer mask to hide it from the dancer. Press-and-hold the Option (PC: Alt) key, and click-and-drag a copy of the layer mask from the dancer layer onto the Hue/Saturation adjustment layer's mask. This replaces the blank mask on the adjustment layer with the mask of the dancer, but has the opposite effect of what we want—it hides the Hue/Saturation adjustment from the background and only affects the dancer. So, go to the Masks panel and click the Invert button to invert the mask, so the color affects the background instead.

STEP 6: RANDOMIZE THE LIGHTING ON THE BACKGROUND TEXTURE

Let's randomize the lighting on that background texture with a cool layer/filter trick. Add a new, blank layer above the others. Press D to set your Foreground and Background colors to their defaults of black and white. Go to Filter>Render>Clouds, then blur this by going to Filter>Blur> Gaussian Blur and enter a setting of 20 pixels. This softens the texture. Change the layer's blend mode to Color Dodge and set the Opacity to 20%. Copy the same layer mask from the Hue/ Saturation adjustment layer to your new layer, so it doesn't show on the dancer.

STEP 7: COPY-AND-PASTE THE FIRE AND SMOKE IMAGE INTO YOUR MAIN IMAGE

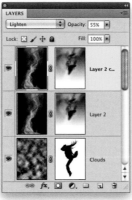

Next, open the cool fire and smoke image and copy-and-paste it into the cover image. Add a layer mask to the layer and paint away most of the fire from the dancer's face and body area, as well as from some of the background. Change the layer blend mode to Lighten and reduce the Opacity to about 55%.

TIP: Whenever you work with background elements like fire and smoke, try pressing Command-J (PC: Ctrl-J) to duplicate the layer and intensify the effect, as I did here. Sometimes it works, and sometimes it doesn't, but it only takes a second to try out.

STEP 8: DOWNLOAD SOME SMOKE BRUSHES

It's time for some more smoke, so I downloaded some free brush presets from Falln-Stock at deviantART (at http://falln-stock.deviantart.com/art/Smoke-Brushes-Set-1-92730901). When you download brush sets, just unzip them to your desktop. Then, double-click on the set to install it into Photoshop. Now, when you go to your Brush Picker, you'll see the newly installed presets at the very bottom of the list.

TIP: Don't forget to check out the brush basics tutorial I did over at www.kelbytraining.com/books/layerscs5.

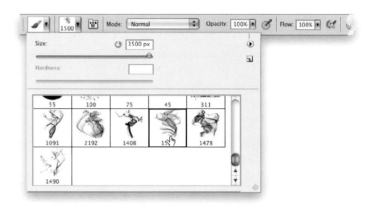

STEP 9: ADD MORE SMOKE

Create a new layer called Smoke, so you'll know what it is, and press D, then X to set your Foreground color to white. Select one of the smoke brushes and click to paint with it on the new layer. You can do this a few times with various brush presets to get different shapes of smoke. Then, reduce the Opacity of the layer to 45%.

TIP: Don't forget you can always go to Edit>Free Transform to change the size of the smoke brush strokes, so they fit into your layout better.

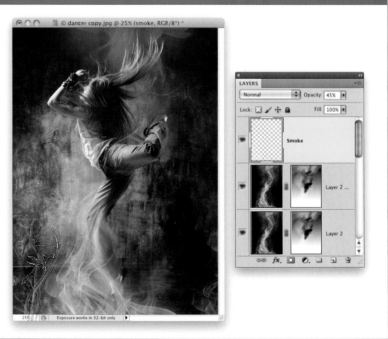

STEP 10: LOAD NEW BRUSHES TO ADD SOME HIGHLIGHTS IN THE HAIR

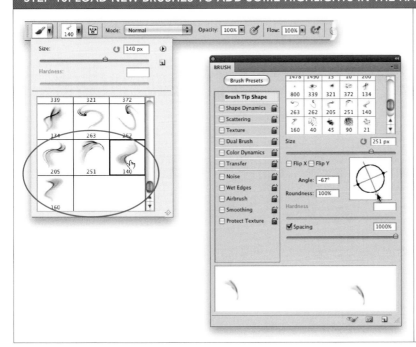

We're going to use another brush set from deviantART called Lighting Brushes (http://Not-a-kitty .deviantart.com/art/Abstract-lighting-brushes-PS7-20838317) to add some wispy highlights to her hair. Once you download and double-click the brush set to install it into Photoshop, go to your Brush Picker and select a brush. I used a combination of the group of brushes you see circled here. Also, go to Window>Brush to open the Brush panel. I turned the Spacing setting to 1000% and I turned off Scattering and Smoothing. Finally, I adjusted the Angle setting to turn the brush so it flowed with the direction of the hair.

STEP 11: PAINT THE HIGHLIGHTS IN THE HAIR

Okay, you're ready to paint some highlights in now. Create a new layer called Hair Highlights. Then, set your Foreground color to R: 247, G: 166, B: 112 (which is a color that's similar to the hair color). Now, click to paint some highlights on the hair. They almost look like they're an extension of the hair, so feel free to paint them anywhere you see stray hair flowing around and switch brushes for a different style. It's a pretty cool effect to enhance the overall dynamic appearance of the hair. When you're done, set the Opacity of the layer to around 80%–85%.

STEP 12: ADD SOME LIGHT STREAKS

It's time for some light streaks. Fortunately, you already know how to do this if you read Chapter 8 on layer styles, because we created a style that was similar. So, select your Brush tool. Go to the Brush Picker and click the small right-facing triangle in the top right to load a new brush set. Choose the Calligraphic Brushes and pick the 20-pixel brush. Create a new layer, set your Foreground color to white, and paint some motion-swirl lines from top to bottom. Make a couple more streak layers. It looks best if you intertwine them with her body, so it looks like they're flowing around her. It's also better if you create them on separate layers, so you can use different colors for each.

STEP 13: ADD OUTER GLOW AND INNER GLOW LAYER STYLES

Double-click on the first streak layer and add an Outer Glow and an Inner Glow layer style to it, using the settings you see here. For both glows, click on the color swatch in the Structure section, and choose the color you'd like the light streak to be (I chose orange, blue, and purple for my light streaks). Click OK when you're done.

STEP 14: ADD A LAYER MASK AND PAINT AWAY PARTS OF THE STREAKS

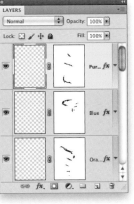

Next, add a layer mask to the first streak layer and paint away parts of the light streak, so it appears as if it's flowing around her body. Repeat Step 13 for each light streak layer you created, changing colors for each one.

STEP 15: ADD SOME SPARKLES AND GLITTER

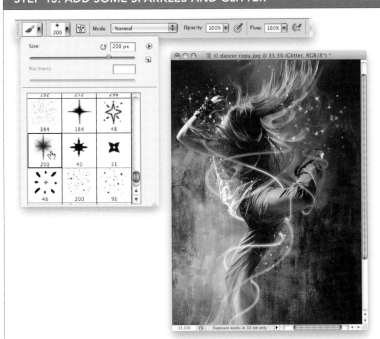

Another effect that's popular for this style of image is glitter and sparkles. Fortunately there's another brush set, by Obsidian Dawn at deviantART (http://browse.devian-tart.com/?qh=&section=&global =1&q=glitter+brushes#/dsyny4), that we can use to help out. Load the Glitter brushes, just like we've done with the other brush sets. In the Brush panel, set the spacing to 265%. Create a new blank layer, set your Foreground color to white, and randomly click around the image to add the sparkles. I used a few different brushes here for some variety.

STEP 16: BLUR THE SPARKLES AND GLITTER TO SOFTEN THE EFFECT

Finally, with the sparkles and glitter layer selected, go to Filter>Blur>Gaussian Blur. Set the Radius to 2 pixels to add a slight blur to the sparkles and glitter so they appear softer. Repeat Steps 15 and 16 a few times to create a few different layers with different sparkle brushes to enhance the appearance and you're done.

Now, I know we covered a lot of ground here. Don't forget that I recorded a video that walks you through this entire tutorial, as well as the rest of the cover graphics (title, wavy layers, background) on the book's downloads site, so check it out if you'd like to see more.

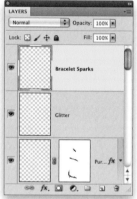

HOW DO I LEARN MORE FROM MATT?

SO YOU WANT TO LEARN MORE FROM THE GUY BEHIND THIS BOOK?

You've probably realized that this isn't really a tutorial. However, if you like my lighthearted, yet to-the-point style (like you see here in this book) and you enjoy learning this way, then here are some other things that I do:

MY PHOTOGRAPHY, PHOTOSHOP, AND LIGHTROOM VIDEOCASTS

I co-host a weekly digital photography videocast called *D-Town TV* (the D stands for Digital) with Scott Kelby. We share everything from camera tips, to shooting advice, studio setups, and lighting techniques, as well as some post-production ideas. With Dave Cross, we also co-host one of the top-rated technology videocasts in the world, *Photoshop User TV*, where we share some of the hottest Photoshop tutorials, tips, and tricks (make sure you laugh at the jokes, even if they're bad). You can find both at http://kelbytv.com. I also teach Adobe Photoshop Lightroom. My weekly videocast and accompanying website (www .lightroomkillertips.com) are quick and to the point.

SOCIAL MEDIA: FACEBOOK AND TWITTER

I keep up with the popular social media sites like Facebook and Twitter. It's a good place to find out what's going on and to keep up with new my new work.

Facebook: www.facebook.com /ThePhotoshopGuy

Twitter: www.twitter.com/Matt Kloskowski

NATIONAL ASSOCIATION OF PHOTOSHOP PROFESSIONALS (WWW.PHOTOSHOPUSER.COM)

This is where I work. So if you like my style, then you'll love NAPP. You get a subscription to *Photoshop User* magazine, which is the premier Photoshop magazine, along with online content, forums, tech support, and discounts from a number of retailers.

I do DVDs, videos, and online training, too. Again presented in a simple, straightforward, and lighthearted way, you'll find my topics span everything from Photoshop, to Lightroom, all the way to Adobe Illustrator. You can find all of it (plus titles from some other awesome trainers, as well) right here.

Contrary to what you'd think after reading the other things that I do, they actually do let me out of the office from time to time (only twice a year, really). These times happen to be at the Photoshop World Conference & Expo, held once on the East Coast and once on the West Coast each year. Not only will you get live training from me, but you can take classes from 30 of my buddies, as well. It's a total Photoshop love fest. You'll love it!

Index